HowExpert Presents

How To Use a 3D Printer

HowExpert with Zachary Hestand

For more tips related to this topic, visit HowExpert.com/3dprinter.

Recommended Resources

- HowExpert.com – Quick 'How To' Guides on All Topics from A to Z by Everyday Experts.
- HowExpert.com/free – Free HowExpert Email Newsletter.
- HowExpert.com/books – HowExpert Books
- HowExpert.com/courses – HowExpert Courses
- HowExpert.com/clothing – HowExpert Clothing
- HowExpert.com/membership – HowExpert Membership Site
- HowExpert.com/affiliates – HowExpert Affiliate Program
- HowExpert.com/writers – Write About Your #1 Passion/Knowledge/Expertise & Become a HowExpert Author.
- HowExpert.com/resources – Additional HowExpert Recommended Resources
- YouTube.com/HowExpert – Subscribe to HowExpert YouTube.
- Instagram.com/HowExpert – Follow HowExpert on Instagram.
- Facebook.com/HowExpert – Follow HowExpert on Facebook.

Table of Contents

Introduction

So you've heard of 3D Printers and you want to find out more about them? Well here's the place to be! I will show you in a 7 step guide what 3d printers are all about, how to use one, and even help you decide which one is right for you!

Chapter 1: Getting Started

1.1 What is a 3D printer?

Well a 3d printer in simplest complex is a printer that makes 3-dimensional objects usually out of plastic. Since we are talking about more consumer based 3D printers, I will stick with the basic type of printer, Fused Deposition modeling (FDM) or Fused filament fabrication (FFF).

What these more complex names mean is basically a machine that will lay down layer after layer of plastic, fusing each layer to the next, ultimately forming the object. To get the picture in your head, think of a hot glue gun how it pushes out that thick goopy glue. Imagine running the hot glue gun in a square, then placing more glue on top of the old glue, and keep doing that until you have a nice little cube.

That is basically what a 3D printer does, at a much more fine level, usually $1/10^{th}$ to $3/10^{th}$ of a millimeter. (Sometimes less for super fine detail!) This entire process is automatic however, as the machine will move to do this processes.

1.2 Can I Use a 3d Printer?

This is the true question many ask. Before jumping into the world of 3D printing, think. Do you patience? 3D printing can be a very long process. Do you have the basic skills of tinkering? The more affordable a printer is, the more likely it will malfunction or have flaws. You must be willing to tinker and try to improve on your printer. Do you have the money?

3D printers can be very expensive, from the printer itself, to the filament (plastic) it uses. Finally, one of the most important parts is, what will you use it for? Many people forget to ask themselves this question. A 3D printer is an amazing tool, and can be used in many different applications. If you plan on buying it just for printing the toys, it may get old after a while.

Many use 3D printers for making replicas of things, props, robotics, or any other hobby. Some people even find success in selling their 3d prints; however this goes into an entirely different subject that will be cover later in this guide. Even if you don't have a hobby application for it yet, then maybe it is time for you to get into a hobby that 3d printing can apply to!

Chapter 2: Buying a 3D Printer

So, you have decided to buy a 3d printer! Or you are at least thinking about buying one. I am not going to lie and say this step is easy, it's not. Finding the right printer for your situation, within the right budget is difficult. You will have to do your homework and look at different printer's prices, reviews, specs, and more.

2.1 Price Ranges

3D printers come in different price ranges, just like anything else. I will break them down into 5 different price ranges to make it easier for those that a very specific budget, and the recommend a printer out of the category to check out.

The first range would be the entry level printers. Printers in this price range will be below $500. This is why they are known as entry level, as it's better to try the cheaper alternative then go full blown into something more expensive.

A lot of these printers however, will come as kits rather than a full assembled version. (For the fully assembled version of a lot of kits will put it outside the entry level range) Building a printer can be good for you though, as you learn exactly how it ticks, and will in the future know what to or not to look for when purchasing a better, more sophisticated printer. Printers in this price range are also made with cheaper parts or designs.

Be wary of that and look for printers will good reviews, as you don't want to get a printer that barely works and have to put even more money into it just to get a print.

For the printer I recommend to check out (everyone in fact, it's more than just a budget printer) is the Wanhao I3 V2. This printer has an amazing build, with strong, metal components, a decent 8inx8inx7in build platform, and overall quality parts.

The Wanhao, after fine tuning has been known to outperform printers 2-3 times its price and is also backed by a huge community of people that own one as well. Coming in at $400, this printer is worth checking out!

The next price ranger is dubbed the "affordable" range. Ranging from $500-$750, these printers are usually better built that entry level printers but are still in the *affordable* range for your average consumer.

However, this is also a very strange price range. The printers are very similar to the entry level printers, but paying an extra $250-$500 would put you on the next range and give you significantly a better printer. The one perhaps advantage over the entry level printers is you can find printers in the price range with enclosures, which can help keep noise down, and printer filament that is sensitive to cooling, such as ABS (What Legos are made of).

For this price range it is tough, but one of the most highly rated printers in this range is the Flash forge Finder, at $500. Yes, it sits right at the edge of going into entry level, and you probably could find a used one for less, but even so, it better suits this range with its enclosure, which may be the only thing it has on the Wanhao.

The 3rd range is known as the mid-range printers. Ranging from $750-$1000, these printers are an amazing example of constantly changing technology, and some consider these printers on the lower end of the "high-end" printers, as they perform amazingly, without costing you an arm and a leg. Printers in this price range truly differ from those in the previous ranges, as they have many different options, better builds, bigger build envelopes, and higher quality printing.

This is also the start of the good plug n play machines; they don't require a lot of maintenance, are extremely easy to use, and work out of the box. I would only recommend these printers though for people who either have previous experience in 3d printing, or know they are going to need this no matter what, as this would be an expensive let down if you end up not liking 3d printing.

For the price ranges printer, I would put out the QIDI Tech I. A metal frame, with a decent 8.8in x 5.9in x 5.9in built area. Coming in at about $700 it is at the lower price range of the tier. A further note though on printers in these ranges. With these plug and play designs; you lose customization that earlier ranges were full of. Some printers in these ranges here on up will still be customizable but for many, that is not the case.

The next range is dubbed the enthusiast level. Costs ranging from $1000-$2000, these printers are for none other than the enthusiasts. These printers are some of the best printers on the market, without paying $2000+ dollars. Zortrax M200 is the winner for this price range with some of the best reviews.

Coming in at $1,935, this printer is truly a plug and play machine. Little or no work is needed to be done (except pulling it out of the box) to get it to print quality objects. Now, I am not putting down the M200 saying it is a bad machine or anything, however this is an example of paying more for plug and play. Yes, this machine is made with much more quality parts than (as if you cannot tell by now, I like referencing it) the Wanhao i3, its build platform is only 5mm taller with the exact same X and Y dimensions. Printers in this price range are a lot of times what set people apart from the tinkers to the just users. You don't or can't tinker with most printers in this price range with how they are built.

If something breaks as well, replacement parts can be outrageous, as most parts here are made specifically for each printer and are not something generic. An example of this is the MakerBot 5th generation Smart Extruder. The extruder itself is quite smart in some cases, having the capability to detect jams, if you run out of filament and more.

If this extruder were to break after its 6 month warranty, it will set you back $200. Be warry of things like this, you don't want to have to save for months and month for example, buy it, and have to pay even more money. Read reviews and information in this price range as well.Now finally, we come to the last price range. These printers are known as premium level printers. These printers are the ones that exceed $2000.

When you buy one of these, you are buying something that usually has features none other has, from huge build areas, special duel extruders, and more over all ease of use. Another relevant printer in this price range is the SLA printer, which uses lasers in a resin to cure an object with extreme detail.

However, I will not go any farther into this form of 3d printing, as the upkeep and cleanup is outrageous in price and mess. These really are not consumer printers so to say, and are better for companies for fine detail prototyping or jewelers. The printer I have selected from this price range is based off of what I have seen and heard about it and is none other than the Raise 3D N2. This printer comes with a full enclosure, a led touch screen, a massive 12in x 12in x 12in build area, dual extruder options as well as more.

This printer also has the capability to print resolutions of .01 compared to the fine detail most printers can print at is .1. This printer also has incredible features such as one of my favorites, print saving on power lose. If you lose power to a printer for most every printer, you "lose" the print, as the only way to continue is to either restart the entire print, or measure and print the remaining parts of the print separately. With the Raise 3D N2, this will not happen!

Now think long and hard about your choice. Your choice will ultimately reflect your experience with 3d printers. If you buy a bad printer, you are in for a rough road ahead of fixing. If you buy a tinker's printer, be prepared to tinker with it for obvious reasons to improve on its original design to make it better. And if you cough up the money for a high end printer, you will likely find it extremely easy, unless this "quality" printer turns out to be a not so quality. Read reviews, as you did this guide. Join groups dedicated to 3d printing and ask questions. All I can say now is, good luck finding your printer!

Chapter 3: Setting up

Wow! You got yourself a 3D printer! Congratulations, this is a huge step into the world of 3D printing for obvious reasons. Now if you're just reading along to see what's up ahead, no worries, you can use the portion of the guide to understand what it will take from you to operate a 3d printer. Now I will do my best do be as detailed as possible, but at the same time I must remain generic, as different printers will have different set ups, and things needed to be done before your first print. Use this as a general guidance only. Follow all documentation given to you as closely as possible, as that will be your true guide on what to do.

3.1 Unboxing

Now we get to the box, the only thing that is holding you back from your 3d printer. Now this is part is very essential and I advise for you to read carefully. The first thing you want to do before unboxing is check the box itself for damage. 3d printers typically do not like to be jarred, hit, etc. as this can damage all sorts of different pieces.

Take pictures of any areas of concern, such as dents, rips, or even if the box looks opened and resealed. This is proof you can use later on if your printer is missing pieces or damaged in any sort of way to get a free replacement/parts. Now before you open the box, look for warnings that tell you not to open the box with a knife or something sharp.

Sometimes the printer components could be right underneath the top, so you don't want to accidently cut some. Once you have it open, take out any paperwork that is usually at the top. Read through it and see if it has any unboxing instructions. If not, continue to pull your printer out carefully in a nice open area. If something doesn't want to come out, check to make sure it doesn't have another piece attached to it.

Now take any Styrofoam out of the way once the printer has been placed. Mission accomplished, it's out of the box, but now there is more to do. Some printers come in a few different pieces for easier shipping, follow directions and assemble it. (Now if you bought an unassembled kit, now you must assemble the entire thing. Good luck.) Some printers might also include shipping bolts to prevent certain pieces from sliding, or tape over end stops to prevent damage. (Most printers are extremely well packed, and have loads of things protecting them so you should look out for things like that.)

Now of course you should have been following the directions supplied by the manufacturer of your printer. Re-read it again and keep looking out for things needed to be done during unboxing/set up. If you miss something, your printer may not work, or could damage itself when turned on. If you believe you have done so, it is time to move onto the next step!

3.2 Calibrating/First Print

Trust me; nothing is more thrilling than your first "test" print. The joy of seeing your printer do its job is amazing! However, you can't just do a test print once it is assembled, there is work to do! You should be following your directions as I have now told you for the umpteenth time, but I will go over what most will basically say.

If you have a 3d printer like most out there, you must go through the hated process of leveling. Leveling your bed is the process of making your printing area (bed) parallel to the nozzle. If you do not do this, it can result in poor bed adhesion and ultimately a failed print.

As long as you print as reasonable sizes, .1-.3mm, you will not need the most perfect leveling, as the printer will in a way compensate for this, as in areas where it is too close, it will end up not being able to extrude a lot of plastic, while in areas where it is too low it will extrude as much as possible, ultimately leveling out to a perfect leveled print. (If this ends up being made into a video series, I will be able to better explain there, so make sure to check if there is one!)

Some printers will not need to have their bed leveled, but if you do and your printer manufacturer doesn't tell you how to, I recommend using a piece of regular printer paper, and starting in the front left corner, moving the back right, back left then from right, making sure there is a tiny bit of resistance as the paper slides under the nozzle. Before you do this, make sure your nozzle was homed in on the Z axis, as it may have been lifted slightly. If you happen to be having issues leveling your bed, check your z axis rods.

Sometimes one side will be lifted or lower slightly more, causing your bed leveling issue. The easiest way to do this is to home all your axis's. Then measure the z axis rod distance from the bottom to where the gantry starts on the side with the end stop.

Now you may as why? Well the side with the end stop is always right, as it will set itself to a set height every time when it hits the end stop. The other z axis rod however, only knows to stop when the end stop on the other side is pressed, so if it had not made it all the way down, it will just stop regardless.

So now, with the measurement from the one z axis rod in mind, measure the other side. Then, manually twist the coupler (What connects the stepper motor to the z axis rod) until it is the same measurement as the other side. Now your axis is level! You may have to check this every once in a while, as one of your z axis stepper motors may be ever so slightly slow, causing it to get out of alignment after so many uses.

Now it is time for your first print! Now many printers will come with the "test file." This is the best option for your first print. Load it up and load your filament as per the directions and start it! Now sit back and enjoy watching your first print come to life. If you start to see plastic peeling from the bed you should probably stop the print as this should not be happening.

Check your bed leveling and temperatures, then try again. However long later when your print is finished, carefully take it off the bed (as you don't want to ruin your first print!) It turned out good hopefully, didn't it? If it didn't happen it is time to check your troubleshooting guide. After this print, usually a small one, it's time to start printing things that you choose!

And we will get to that later on in the guide. Now, more work will be required sadly, as test printers are usually made by the printer gods themselves. They are perfectly tweaked gcode to always work, but if you go straight into printing something else, you will have issues. Follow the rest of the guide to understand how to prepare your printer so you don't get prints with issues!

Chapter 4: Downloading Models

So you have successfully printed your first test model! Or maybe you are still just reading ahead of time, either way we are now at the step of finding your own models to print! This isn't as it seems however, as there are a few things you may run into while doing this that can cause or get you in A LOT of trouble. Don't you worry about it though, ill cover anything you may run into on this path!

4.1 Where Can I get Models From?

Well, there are many places you can download .stl files (the file type used for 3d printers). One of the best known website is Thingiverse, a website owned by MakerBot. Users from all over the world can upload their models to the website and share them. You can find the most simplistic things on Thingiverse such as a hinge to the most complex things like a model of a T-Rex skeleton!

Some people even allow customization of their files through Thingiverse's customization app to be able to change sizes, lettering etc. Another good website is YouMagine, owned by Ultimaker. Their website is similar to Thingiverse with lots of variation in designs and things to print.

Now you may be asking, are there any other websites? Well yes, there are plenty more. I only chose these two for 3 reasons: The websites are reliable and you are not at risk of downloading viruses, most of the models are 3d printable and all the models are free. The 3d printable part I will get to later, and the free part I will hit now.

Many professional designers will make amazing designs, (like a replica of the millennium falcon that opens up to the inside!) And then turn around and sell the files for tons of money. Thingiverse and YouMagine don't allow people to sell the models through their website, so anything on there will always be free! So just search up what you need and pick the best design that fits your needs (or wants)!

Worst scenario is you can't find exactly what you are looking for. This is when you can find a 3D modeler to make it for you. If it something extremely small and easy, you may be able to find someone in a 3d printer group to make one for free, but if your idea is a full scale power armor suit from Fallout 4, you are going to need to find a professional designer, and a few hundred to thousand dollars to pay them! (Okay, you probably won't be designing a full scale suit, as those are expensive to just print, let alone design. If you're idea is say a model of the super bowl trophy, it will probably cost close to $20).

4.2 What Does Ripping From a Game Mean?

Well in simple terms, 3d games use 3d models to be the game. People will "rip" these 3d models from the game and turn them into a .stl file. This may sound really cool, but at the same time is risky. 3D printers have limitations on what they can print; too much details or complicated structures or overhangs will cause the print to fail, even with the most fine-tuned settings. When people design models from scratch, they take into account that a 3d printer must be able to print this, and optimize the file to be printed in ways such as cutting it into smaller pieces, removing unnecessary details, etc.

If you notice the ripped 3d model of a Honda motorcycle, you will see complicated details such as the spokes, engine and more. This design is likely over complicated for your typically printer and will not turn out anywhere close to what you would like to look like. Now I am not saying something like this is not printable, you can try, but don't say I didn't warn you. This kind of print would be more suitable for a more detailed printer such as an SLA printer, but even then it may be iffy.

4.3 Commercial Use

So now you are ready to start selling your printer objects to earn some money. Now some people are good at this, and find something that sells good but there is a problem. You will likely be downloading these models off of a free site such as Thingiverse.

You must pay extremely CLOSE attention to tags such as if it's allowed to be used for commercial use (sell it). In some cases you can just sell it free, others you must give credit, and others you cannot. Even if you bought the design from a website, you must make sure it is allowed to sell them. A great way to avoid all these problems though are to just design your own models, as then you own all the rights to them or have someone else design for you!

Now if neither of these sound appeasing, the final way to avoid legal problems is to just open a 3d shop that prints what is given. (For example 3dhubs does a "Hub" where users upload a .stl file to the website and by formulas you set; it tells them how much it will cost them. This way, you are technically selling the file, even if it can't be used for commercial use. Now this isn't always the most solid way to go about doing it either, some people will dispute this way, but you are unlikely to run into any problems.

Chapter 5: Filament

Okay, most companies give you a maybe a 10 meter test spool of filament. This is usually just enough to print the test print, and if you are following the 3d model downloading portion, you probably are about to start printing something more. This is where you must buy your own filament. Now I will be explaining _MY OPINION_. My filament may work for you but it may not, so I advise for you to read into more reviews of the different brands.

5.1 Filament Types

The most basic filament around would probably be Polylactic Acid (PLA). This is most likely what your sample filament was. The filament usually prints around 200°C to 215°C. It is has good layer adhesion and isn't affected too much by cooling, however it still needs it. It also can be printed without a heated bed. This is also one of the cheaper filament types. A downside though is its lower temperature causes it to warp it in just a hot summer day.

Another common filament is Acrylonitrile butadiene styrene (ABS). This is the same plastic that Lego Bricks are made out of, so it is a very strong plastic. It printers at about 20°C PLA.The downsides though are it requires a heated bed and is very susceptible to warping, as without an enclosure, breezes can make your part cool unevenly causing the layers to warp and not bond correctly. This filament is general not good for beginners are is can be a true challenge. But if you can successfully print it, you have an incredibly strong part.

The 3rd filament I would recommend is Polyethylene terephthalate (PETG) [and yes, I know these are hard names, nobody actually uses the full name anyways.] This filament is like the perfect combination I would say. It is quite easy to print like PLA, as it has amazing layer adhesion. It prints at about the same temperatures as ABS, but doesn't require a heated bed or an enclosure to keep the cooling perfect. This filament also is incredibly strong, and has a bit of flex as well. This filament is overall an amazing choice for any project.

Now there are other types of filament such as Ninja Flex, a rubbery very flexible filament, TPU, Nylon, and more but a lot of these filaments are either much more advanced, unneeded, or I don't have enough reliable information to recommend them.

5.2 Filament Brands and Prices

So now I have listed 3 different types of filament, but now is where to buy said filament from. I am more of a budget person, so I do not like to spend $50 for a .5kg roll of plastic. There are many brands out there, but these 3 are the ones I have either heard the best reviews about or have used with great results.

Now we go to Inland filament. This filament, a product of the computer store "Microcenter" is widely thought to be rebranded eSun filament. No matter what it is, I have found that its PLA and PETG turn out amazing prints, as long are you tune your printer settings correctly. (I can't help you there, as spools vary and so do printers) The filament can be ordered from microcenter.com and shipped or picked up directly.

If you live close to a microcenter, I would advise you to buy the filament online and the have it pick up at store. This is because the filament in store is actually a few dollars more expensive then online, so you save some money. The PLA filament costs around $15 a kilogram, while the Petg costs around $18. (I cannot say more for the Abs as I have never used it) All in all, this is one the best cheap filaments.

The next brand is known as Hatchbox. I have used their Pla and it creates amazingly smooth objects. The spools even come in a nice cardboard box that can be used to store your tools and more. This filament can be found on Amazon and a few other retailers, but the problem is the filament is extremely popular. The Pla can usually be found on amazon from $20 to $25 depending on the colors.

The weird colors that nobody buys will always be less than the basics such as white. Overall I have found that Hatchbox also has a better filament diameter compared to inland, which is the reason for these smoother finishes. Now I cannot speak for the Petg, which runs close to $34 on amazon, as the price has always steered me clear of it.

The final brand is Maker Geeks. I have yet to use their filament, but have heard many good reviews about it. They sell filaments such as clear, to even special Pla that is much stronger than the original or even abs. Their filament costs around $18.50, with some of their specialty ranging higher. A good trick to do is if you need bulk, for low costs and don't care about the color is to buy from their "grab bag." For $36 you will get 2 random color rolls of whatever type of filament you choose (with the exception of Raptor PLA, which will add +$15) and occasionally they will even go to $60 for 4 rolls, which saves you $12.

Now your choice of filament is entirely up to you. Ask around people in printer groups what they like or use. Just remember though, just like with 3d printers, the most expensive option is not always the best choice.

Chapter 6: Software

Okay, now you have your printer, models, and plastic. What is next? Well you can't just throw a 3d model into a 3d printer, as it does not understand that format, it much be converted into a file known as gcode for it to print. In these following steps I will show you what to do.

6.1 Slicer Software

The program that converts a 3d model into a gcode file is known as a slicer program. What it does is "slices" the 3d model into layers, with each layer containing information telling the printer simple commands such as, move here, extrude this much, heat to this temperature. So in reality, gcode is not a form of a 3d model, it is just a huge list of commands that form a 3d model.

Now some printers must use special gcode for their printers only, so sometimes you are stuck using one type of slicer software. However most printers are open allowing you to switch freely. Many slicer software offer different things, some even cost money, but when it comes down it, they all do the basic function of converting stl files to gcode.

Now in slicer software, you will have many options to change settings, which is where fine tuning comes in. Temperature, infill, shells, speed and more all is to be adjusted before you export your gcode to your 3d printer. If you need help trouble shooting something, Simplify3D offers an amazing guide, and offers things to change to fix the problems.

6.2 What Slicer Should I Use?

Well, if your printer requires your stock slicer, sorry but you are stuck with it, unless you are good with coding and lots of other goodies. If your printer doesn't need a special slicer, I have 3 different slicer softwares for you to choose from.

The first one is known as Cura. Cura is run by the makers of ultimaker 3d printers. Their software offers many different settings with a simplistic layout. If you only want to see basic settings, you can choose that, or go deeper into and change little tiny things. Many printer companies even offer special "profiles" (settings) for their printer. This program is also free and can be downloaded from ultimaker.com.

The second program is known as Slic3r. (Pretty easy to figure out it's a slicer program right?) Slic3r is an independently run slicer. It offers many advanced options such as cutting objects into smaller pieces, and many more. The only downside I can think of it is it looks older than and not as smooth as many of the new slicer softwares around today. But do not let that fool you; it is still an incredible capable and good slicer.

The final slicer I have on this list is called Simplify3D and by no means is this program simple. Simplify3D I would say has the most options and settings than any other slicer program today. With its ability to add customized supports, switch profiles and settings mid print and more, it by far puts itself near the top of all slicers. There is a catch to this amazing slicer though, one that will set you back $150. Yes, this is one of the few slicers that are not free. This slicer is by no means for beginners, as you would never need such a program when learning. Now, for more professional users, or people that need extreme details and fine tunings, this would fit you quite well.

Now choosing a slicer isn't really that hard, most do the exact same thing. You just have to try them out and see which works better for your needs. Most slicers don't care what printer you are using and printers usually don't care what slicer you use, as long as they both use the same gcode, they can't tell a difference.

6.3 How to Use the Slicer

By now you must have at least chosen a slicer to check out. Using a slicer is fairly simple. For beginners, you will want to stick in the basic section. I cannot go too deep in to how to use the slicer, as they vary from each, but basically you will import your model.

Then you will change the settings for the model, such as the infill, the number of perimeters, etc. Next you will either export the gcode to an SD card and insert that straight into your printer or just print from your computer. Now, I would recommend using an SD card if possible, as if your computer performs an update, crashes, or the wire becomes unplugged, you will lose all your progress on your 3d printer and have to restart.

If your printer for some reason doesn't have an SD card slot, you can always use something like Octoprint, which is a raspberry pi that will plug into your usb slot and act as a mini computer. You can send gcode wirelessly, and not have to worry about your pc shutting off, as the gcode is then saved on the pi. Octoprint also gives you options to view your print while away if you have a camera and even remotely stop your printer! As I said before, printers vary, so read up on your printer on how it accepts gcode files.

Chapter 7: Modding

Now look at it this way. We all strive for perfection. Many prints can get some really amazing prints right off the bat, but of course those printers cost lots of money. If you want to get better prints, you probably will have to tinker with your printer to get them.

7.1 When Should I mod?

Well that is entirely up to you. If you see problems begin to form or see others with the same printers who are getting better results, its problem about time. Some people though choose to mod right off the bat, even if there are no immediate problems present. This future proofs them. It also depends on what you are printing.

Personally, I print items that need fine details and to be smooth, so I don't have to do lots of post printing work. Now if you are just doing lots of prototyping, then you may not care about lines showing. Sometimes printers are also made with design flaws.

For example, my Wanhao printer, the top beam sits too low to be able to get all 180mm of z height, so I modded it to lift it up more. Modding also depends on what kind of printer you have. Most Prusa style printers are very moddable, as their core printer they are based off of uses printed parts to function!

Now the more expensive printers that are built in enclosures, such as the MakerBot, ultimaker and more, are harder to mod, as the way they are designed really doesn't allow for it. Prusa style printers most of the time can be completely disassembled and reassembled to allow for modding, while as more expensive ones, it is much harder to take apart. This doesn't mean you cannot mod more expensive printers; it's just usually harder and sometimes not ever even needed.

7.2 What Should I Mod?

Once again, that is entirely up to you. What you mod is based off of what you can feasibly mod on your printer, and why you should. As the old saying goes, if it's not broke, don't fix it. (Now, it doesn't have to actually be broke, for example, changing a nozzle to a better one is "fixing" a broke nozzle).

Some examples of modding would be z-bracing. Prusa style printers can be unstable near the top, causing z banding, where the layers form deep grooves every so often. A simple solution is to have z braces (rods) attach to the top of the printer, down to the bottom from of the printer. This makes the printer extremely rigid and prevents wobble.

Another example would be fixing bent or crooked z rods. Sometimes in transit the z rods, (what make the printer rise) can get bent. Or when assembled, the rods are nearly impossible to make straight unless it is secured from both sides. If the rod is not attached to the printer at the top, it can wiggle, once again causing z banding.

To fix this, you can install flex couplers instead of solid couplers. A coupler is a small usually plastic of metal piece that attaches the rod to the stepper motor. Flex couplers can bend to compensate for this wiggle, and force it to stop.

Another thing people will mod is their nozzle. Sometimes printer companies use a really crappy nozzle, or bad nozzle set up.

With some extra work, you can switch out the nozzle type, or change from a direct drive set up to a Bowden setup or vis versa.

(A direct drive extruder set up uses a stepper motor right on top of the nozzle heater. This pulls filament to it and pushes it directly into the heater. A Bowden set up, most commonly used on delta style printers will pull filament usually from the bottom the printer or near the top, and push it through a tube that leads to the heater block. Both set ups have their advantages and dis advantages)

What you mod is entirely up to you as I have said before. Usually you can find a community dedicated to your printer, or a similar printer, and they can assist you in how to mod it or what to mod.

When modding though, pay close attention to the amount of money you spend. If you buy a $100 printer but put $500 of mods into it, why didn't you just by a $600 printer that wouldn't need these mods? (Unless of course there was some other reason for doing this).

About the Expert

I am currently a student who makes who works with 3d printing. I have worked with my specific 3d printer, the Wanhao i3 V2 for about a year now and have enjoyed every moment of it. I found 3D printing extremely hard but fascinating from the beginning however I believe anyone who even has the slightest interest should learn more about it and see if they can "connect" with it. I mainly got into 3d printing by seeing people make these incredible things, and I thought to myself, I have to do this. Now, that dream has come true, and I have the ability to work on amazing projects for clients and myself alike, such as BB-8 from Star Wars, the Force Awakens.

HowExpert publishes quick 'how to' guides on all topics from A to Z by everyday experts. Visit HowExpert.com to learn more.

Recommended Resources

- HowExpert.com – Quick 'How To' Guides on All Topics from A to Z by Everyday Experts.
- HowExpert.com/free – Free HowExpert Email Newsletter.
- HowExpert.com/books – HowExpert Books
- HowExpert.com/courses – HowExpert Courses
- HowExpert.com/clothing – HowExpert Clothing
- HowExpert.com/membership – HowExpert Membership Site
- HowExpert.com/affiliates – HowExpert Affiliate Program
- HowExpert.com/writers – Write About Your #1 Passion/Knowledge/Expertise & Become a HowExpert Author.
- HowExpert.com/resources – Additional HowExpert Recommended Resources
- YouTube.com/HowExpert – Subscribe to HowExpert YouTube.
- Instagram.com/HowExpert – Follow HowExpert on Instagram.
- Facebook.com/HowExpert – Follow HowExpert on Facebook.

www.ingramcontent.com/pod-product-compliance
Lightning Source LLC
La Vergne TN
LVHW092010050326
832904LV00001B/2

THE FUTURE OF TECHNOLOGY IN EDUCATION

HOW ARTIFICIAL INTELLIGENCE WILL TRANSFORM THE LEARNING AND TEACHING PROCESS FOREVER

Harib Shaqsy

COPYRIGHT NOTICE

Table of Contents

8

Introduction

I have been interested in introducing better and advanced technology including Artificial Intelligence (AI) devices to schools for many years, for bettering teaching and learning while creating an environment of fun and excitement while learning and teaching.

I wish I could have had a good support from the organization in order to showcase many of my ideas of which I believed would have helped to improve the teaching and learning to a much more efficient and fun for both teachers and students.

A couple of years ago, I had a chance to at least showcase a few of my ideas to the educational institution.
I and the team members had also worked on one of these projects for nearly a year.
This project was an online system for books including its application, but this is not as an Artificial Intelligence system, it is just a simple script for uploading our curriculum books for classes from class one to class twelve. These books

were all available online and can be read online easily using either a laptop, a Tablet or an iPad. Plus it has many options, I call this project "The open gate to the next big thing".

The script can include many features such as embedding creative interactive curriculum such as animations, videos, audios, quizzes and many other features.

This was simple but fun for both students and teachers.

The aim of this project is to start from a simple useful tool then to a better and bigger system including AI devices and IoT (Internet of Things).

But unfortunately, this project was paused for many months for some reason.

The project was an ongoing and was requiring a full conversion of source from the regular Adobe Flash based to an HTML version for use with Tablets, iPads and Mobile Phones. After many months at least the conversion of most books where done and uploaded.

We need to start introducing AI and IoT devices to schools from now. There is no better time than now.

One of the reasons I wrote this book is to share some of my knowledge to the public of which I have achieved through many research, readings, seminars, webinars, online video trainings and workshops.

This researched information includes my opinion and some from IT experts and educators around the world of which I have referenced them in this book.

This information is for those who are interested in learning more about the effect of Artificial Intelligence in education and other technology and would like to implement these tools including AI in their educational system.

I want to see that many educational institutions implement these tools and technology in schools in order to create a better learning environment and to create a meaningful and enjoyable learning experience.

Books are great tools for passing knowledge to the next generations.

Artificial Intelligence known as AI, is a field that has a long history but has continued to grow and change. Even before involving education directly, it has been used to create tools which are also used by teachers and students in many teachings.

It is a powerful driving force in changing humanity by assisting educators, businesses and people generate exciting, creative learning environment, products and services, make critical decisions, and attain major goals, plus helping teachers to teach in a more effective way and students to learn in a more effective way.

In schools of some countries of this world, students are even using the help of AI devices such as Amazon Alexa to ask questions and get answers, this is one of the many other tools.

This is the reason why organizations keep hiring AI experts at a jaw-dropping speed.

For example, the median salary of an AI developer in the US and other developed countries is not less than $80,000 based on payscale.com. Virtually all great tech companies run an artificial intelligence project and are ready to cash out millions of dollars to assist in completing the project.

Approximately 13.6 million jobs will emerge in the AI field in the next decade. However, there is a staggering shortage of talent in AI, and especially when it comes to educational system, the need for improving learning and teaching is increasing and therefore, using tools such as Artificial Intelligence (AI) is of great importance.

I came to know that, there are less than 10,000 people in the world with the skill set sufficient to carry out a significant research.

Artificial Intelligence (AI) technology is highly popular in our daily lives. It has applications in different sectors right from gaming, media to finance, education and also the state-of-the-art research industries from medical diagnosis, robotics, and quantum science.

The important reason why I believe internet will be one new technological teaching method to any school because internet has reach the mature and popular stage to let any students accept to use this method to learn in the future. It seems that any school need to spend time to prepare how to change to adopt this IT and internet new technological educational method from traditional lecturer face-to-face oral teaching method of which expects future student emotion and teaching challenges to be solved successfully. The most important reason, IT educational method will attract many students to choose the school to study. Because internet had reached the mature stage and it will be one popular teaching acceptance tool to any students. Research and practice have shown that when the students' work is structured as sequences of challenges, models, training, performance, and feedback, students respond with interest. As a result, they learn to take charge of their learning because the would-be performers do not enjoy and benefit from the lengthy upfront lectures. Instead, they need some explicit instruction on a "need-to-know" basis so they can begin to see knowledge and skills as the tools to accomplish a specific task or a set of functions within a complex performance (Wiggins and Tighe, 2005).

This book will give a comprehensive overview of the technological changes in education in the near future, with particular focus on artificial intelligence (AI) and automation and the effects they will have on teaching and learning process. People won't get stuck into nitty-gritty details, that is the job of other, more specialized, books. Instead, you will build a strong foundation of knowledge of how AI will change the future of education and also how some of the most disruptive industries will change how people live and work along with the many opportunities it will create.

As technology becomes increasingly faster, cheaper and more capable, those who resist and fight will only prolong the inevitable pain and misery while those who accept it and use it to their advantage will enjoy a rewarding and prosperous life.

The best place to start is by learning as much as you can, such as with this book. You are also never too old to learn or retrain; as people will see, those who are taking online degrees are on average in their mid-30s, have at least one child and are in full employment. There is no excuse. There is also no excuse to delay. As AI in the workplace gets exponentially more common, those who are the least prepared will be the first to go. Can you afford to be that person? I know I can't, so without further ado, let's address the elephant in the room.

Artificial Intelligence in Education Today

Artificial intelligence has, and still is, been viewed as a future concept. In the eyes of a regular person, AI is an advanced concept that involves futuristic abilities and cutting-edge designs. The reality, though, is that AI is very much alive and already present in the lives of many. You're using AI whenever you use interactive software. Robots, which were a futuristic concept decades ago are also present in the modern world; they are vacuuming homes, telling cars where to go, working in storages and moving a load from point A to point B;

AI technology has been steadily developing and shaping into useful gadgets for nearly two decades, and it also found its place in education. Distant learning, online learning, digital learning, and many others, are the main purposes for which AI software is being used. Looking into the future of technology in education, I see a discrepancy in the thought process. We're all inclined to picture the future changes in education as revolutionary, groundbreaking, and transformative. Yet, most of us forget that even very basic elements of digital resources are yet to become a common standard in an average classroom. Rather than picturing an out-of-this-world concept of technologically advanced education, I'm more inclined to look into the real picture. I see that the revolutionary progress we are all hoping for will first require universal implementation of today's achievements. Only when advanced technologies become common to most classrooms, and when educational systems have worked with them long enough to take them to the next level, transformation towards highest levels of learning will be possible. In this sense, let me present you with the very basics of AI and its use in education.

I've come across arguments that self-learning and artificial intelligence may be on the path of taking over the teaching process, other jobs and careers. To answer this questions, let's answer two more important questions:

● Which are the tasks that a computer can do that a human can't?

- Which are the skills that only people possess, that are irreplaceable by machines?

According to the Theory of evolution of computer-based systems, computers are to complete tasks that would normally require human intelligence. Siri is a pretty good example of artificial intelligence and a quite obvious example of how AI is becoming common in the modern world.

I see two polarizing views regarding the future of artificial intelligence:
- Artificial intelligence might lead to destruction;
- Artificial intelligence might lead to salvation;

Machine learning is a very basic form of artificial intelligence. You can see it everywhere all around you, namely in form of interactive software made to make our daily lives easier. To phrase it simply, I see machine learning as a process where the system self-upgrades at performing tasks by repeating actions.

Is AI Destructive?

The biggest fear surrounding artificial intelligence is that it will turn against its creators and try to control the world. I like to call this "The Matrix scenario". Those who fear AI believe that it will try to dominate the world. But is this fear justified?

In my efforts to answer this question, I came across a Microsoft experiment. Microsoft used an artificial intelligence bot to post tweets. The bot learned from other Tweeter users and formulated posts based on this knowledge. Here, I learned that the biggest danger from allowing AI to learn from people is the very fact that it's learning from people. The Microsoft's bot became consumed with aggressive, racist ideas. This happened because of the quality of the information it gathered from other human users. Needless to say, the experiment went infamously and taught us one important lesson: AI may become aggressive if exposed to aggressive role models.

Although far into the future (or is it?), the artificial intelligence that we create will, like a growing child, absorb and repeat equally positive and negative examples that we provide. This includes, but not limited to, racism, sexism and other anti-social ideas that we, as mankind, don't want to promote.

My final conclusion on this topic is that AI can become destructive, and that is an option to account for. But is it worth abandoning the entire concept and giving the possible benefits to the education of society? I don't believe so, as I put my faith in the vision of creators.

Is AI going to replace teachers?

In theory, AI could assume the teaching role, hence replacing teachers in classrooms. If a software can test, access, communicate, and provide feedback, perhaps there's truly no need for a human teacher. Or, is it?

I came across highly advanced studies that claim that it would be hypothetically possible to install chips inside the student's brains, which will further allow the AI to study the student's personality. Based on gathered data, the AI will provide a personalized teaching approach. Forming such an algorithm of artificial intelligence would prospectively enable it to create lesson plans for each individual student.

Despite this information, I don't believe that human teachers are, or should be replaceable. Education is far more than absorbing information. It also serves for students to develop moral systems, emotional intelligence, and social intelligence. My thought on the matter is that AI won't replace teachers. Here's why:

AI can assist, but not lead.

The data collected by the Artificial Intelligence can help teachers learn more about student's qualities. Ultimately, students need to be taught to be empathetic, loving and open-minded. Artificial intelligence has a role in this but it's questionable whether or not eliminating authentic human contact from the learning process helps students form the right social-emotional skills. As adults, these students will live and work surrounded by people. When engaging with a teacher, students gain a leader. They learn not only about problem-solving but also conflict-solving.

Independent thinking is teacher's work

Human teachers are essential for a traditional classroom, as they help students learn how to analyze and create their own conclusions. Thanks to human contact with teachers, students are able to develop important cognitive skills like critical thinking and problem-solving.

Social norms and employment

Teachers also help children adopt social norms and shape their behaviors to be able to function in their social environments. While economists conclude that teachers make an important contribution to lifelong learning, to improve test scores and pregnancy rates in teenagers, they also significantly affect student's lifetime earnings. In fact, some estimations state that teachers contribute to students earning up to $66,000 throughout their working career.

So, what are the benefits of the use of digital resources in the classroom?

Digital resources enhance the classroom.

Digital resources like high-quality instructional videos, crowdsourced lesson plans as well as the blended skill learning improve the lesson quality and offer a multi-dimensional approach to common topics.

The blended learning approach to education is where instruction is augmented by digital resources. It is becoming a standard in many developed countries. Nowadays, AI-powered essay grading software scans can assess the student's work, while the hybrid software systems are able to communicate with systems and tools that are technology-based. AI also provides high-quality and fast feedback, which streamlines the teaching process and allows the teacher to put in more effort into more creative aspects of learning.

There is also AI-influenced progress in the area of supporting the student's emotional development. Artificial systems are capable of measuring metacognition, which is the student's awareness of how well they are learning. In the future, AI systems are going to be able to analyze emotional states in students and identify the exact areas or times when they need additional support. While this might take away from the key role of the human teacher, it also helps maximize the learning process. Artificial intelligence can extend the abilities and the reach of teachers and education systems. It can free up more teacher's time from time-consuming activities, allowing them to directly communicate with students. You see, I don't think that the most important question is whether or not teachers are replaceable by the AI. I believe that pinpointing the exact spots where students need more support, guidance, and instruction is far more important.

Neuroscience of learning

A human brain is designed to learn. The human brain has a natural thirst for knowledge. Self-directed exploration and experimenting are some of the basic ways in which the human brain learns.

Why so many students struggle at school? It is because there is a mismatch between their interests and the curriculum design. There is also a discrepancy between the way in which the education is designed and in the way in which the human brain is naturally built to learn.

The AI has the endless possibility to design the learning materials in ways that are natural to the human brain. The learning centers in the brain release endorphins during the process of learning, which means that a human brain needs to find joy and pleasure in learning. In fact, the release of endorphins is a "U-shaped line". This means that students find the most pleasure in learning materials that are in-between familiar and pleasurable. If students are presented with contents that are completely unfamiliar they are unable to enjoy them and therefore unable to adopt them. However, if the students are also presented with overly familiar contents, they become bored.

When students are presented with the exact measure content difficulty as to be partially new and partially familiar for the student to be able to relate, the learning doesn't only become pleasurable. It also becomes addictive. Students need to approach the learning process with a certain level of confidence and security. To provide that, teachers and content creators must initially shape the lessons to whatever is closest to the student's knowledge. Gradually introducing new elements that contrast and challenge the former, increasing the difficulty and the level of challenges that these learning matters pose, results in more interest and motivation for learning. On the one hand, students feel successful because they can understand the matter to a certain degree. This initial understanding allows them to study the little familiar elements and eventually learn them. As this process continues to repeat students eventually develop an "addiction to learning". However, lessons are not designed in this way. Curriculum creators and teachers fail to understand that students need to associate new content with something familiar. Instead, they shape lessons in a way which presents only new content for the student. Students are then unable to grasp the relevance and the importance of a lesson. Teachers automatically assume that students will learn because they are expected to learn and because it's one of their duties. However, true learning is more than just absorbing information and reproducing when asked for during tests and exams. Students, in order to create true knowledge, must deeply understand and analyze the contents on multiple levels and draw conclusions, create habits, and skills from the resources and the contents they are presented with.

With the ability to deeply personalize the learning process, artificial intelligence will, in one point of time be able to identify the elements that are closest to the student's knowledge and experience and present the contents in a way that relatable to a student, in a way that helps students see the lesson is something important. This is deeply individual and depends on a person's unique experiences and cultural background. For example, a lesson on World War II won't have the same impact on students of different geographic backgrounds. Those who are geographically closer to areas where the war had the most effect will clearly be more motivated to learn. Those students who haven't experienced cultural references on the matter will be less motivated to learn about it. In this circumstance, a good teacher will find a way to bring the matter close to the student by referencing historical events from their own cultural backgrounds with which student has an emotional relationship. However, I'm not talking about most teachers here. Millions of students every day or presented with lessons that they can't emotionally associate with, but are still expected to adopt. When presented with data about students' individual experiences in backgrounds, artificial intelligence software can draw from these experiences and offer relatable elements to students also known as the 'initial successes'.

One experiment with robots using artificial intelligence showed that a robot quickly abandoned the activities that didn't serve many purposes, replacing them with purposeful actions. By gradually learning this, the robot started emulating the similar learning process of a baby in terms of developing hand-eye coordination. As the repeated activities became boring over time and no longer offered anything new, the robot started adopting new operations.

The reason that the students fall behind in class is that there are no one-size-fits-all in terms of shaping lessons. Every student is an individual, and the result of applying the same method of teaching to a group of 30 students is that more than half of students become disengaged.

For an average teacher, it is simply too much work to individualize the content and to personalize the lessons for every student. Here enters the Artificial Intelligence with its ability to streamline the lessons, handle the assessment scores and planning and leave the teacher with more time to interact with the student. It leaves the teacher more time to talk to each student and offer those experiences that are relatable to the learning matter learn, the student's individual properties, and to direct the student towards the areas they're most talented in. Within this context, the artificial intelligence is somewhat of a teacher's assistant.

Three levels of artificial intelligence

Not all Artificial Intelligence is the same. Nowadays, scientists are working with the very basic forms of AI and trying to learn how to give it the best form of application. Here are the three basic forms of AI:

Rote Learning

Rote learning is the very basic knowledge of information. It answers the basic questions such as what is the capital of a certain country or which language is spoken in a certain country. To provide answers to these questions artificial intelligence doesn't have to do anything more complex than simply storing and reproducing information. However, students retain very little of this information as they don't have a much emotional relationship with it and they most often forget this information after 'cramming' for the test.

 Spaced repetition is one way of the overcome this obstacle. If students are repeatedly tested after a certain period of time and reminded of this information they are more likely to retain it long term. With reproductive learning, students reread and highlight what they identify as important formation. With active learning, students use flashcards and quizzes.

Knowing exactly what students don't know in the current time and presenting them with the information they need for active learning is impossible for a regular teacher. However, for machine learning, it becomes an almost trivial task. One of the amazing achievements of artificial intelligence is the creation of interactive flashcards. Flash cards offer multimedia contents and they're interactive.

Using interactive flashcards, students are presented with information that is designed in a way to entertain and please their minds.

Generative AI

Generative AI can actually gather the information from the students, like answers to simple questions and playing instruments, and it can instantly give its own feedback on how correct the student's answers are. This approach is applicable to a wide range of topics from mathematics to music and even arts.

Generative AI in the classroom provides the answer to the question "what" by offering personalized machine learning. Moreover, it provides the answer to the question "why" with the personalized group projects. The second is up to the teacher and it's the teachers the most important task.

Integrative AI

Integrative AI blends simulated virtual reality (digital learning interface) and gesture recognition (user's response to tasks). In this form, AI can be even used to teach children martial arts or sign language. This form blends with the previous two, offering a highly economical and fast method of teaching through students' individual capacities, personal experiences, the right types of content and challenges.

Why AI is the future of education

Throughout the evolution and research of machine learning in the forms in which it exists today, experts have focused their studies on technological and educational aspects. Among those who have studied the advance of learning in the computerized environment, the notion of the success of machine learning appears as one of the key points of the assessment of the effectiveness of machine learning programs in general.

In the setting of the study of machine learning, the success of the machine process is, in the eyes of many, a result of the number of factors. From the very beginning of the machine learning platform design, and the design of the machine learning environments, it has become evident that the learning outcomes depend on the overall experience of the digital environment. Not only the content but also the way in which the information is presented, systems that enable the interaction of participants in the educational process, all the way to the technological foundations of the instructional design of the computerized learning platform, are elements that, according to many, affect the learning outcomes.

In recent years, studying factors that influence the success of computerized learning has been intensified. Numerous studies resulted in pointing out a variety of different impact factors, their classification, and systematization. What makes the task of examining computerized education in its entirety, its evaluation and performance measurement so complicated and demanding is the very nature of the concept of AI and machine learning. Computerized education, as a term, in all its various forms and manifestations, is the result of interconnected achievements and the work of experts of several different sciences and scientific fields. Namely, machine learning is a kind of hybrid, a blend of technology and psychology, as well as the economy. The two polarizing scientific areas, which historically have always been connected in many ways, are united in this scientific field as never before. Machine learning cannot be separated from technology, due to the technological foundation which provides the basics on which psychological and educational elements are being added to. The educational nature of the concept requires the application of knowledge in all areas, from the creation of the learning environment to the creation of learning content, the interaction of participants, the administrative work of administrative officials and teaching staff. Equally important in this process is the psychological element, which provides and studies mental processes that take place in the process of computerized education. Experts from the fields of psychology provide a key contribution to the development of machine learning through the study of the process of learning, motivation, measuring various factors that impact and condition this process: the administration, teaching staff, students to content design and interface design and the instruction provided with it.

Designing and operation of AI-based learning systems requires the constant collaboration of various scientific fields, in order to produce a quality designed program that is effective for its purpose. Like any other form of education, AI learning aims at building, shaping knowledge, skills, and habits in different contexts and professional fields. It also has tasks that are equivalent to teaching tasks in general, which are both educational and functional tasks. Throughout the development of computerized learning, including its shortcomings and limitations, these key elements mustn't be excluded from the big picture. For this reason, effective machine learning requires a unified, multidisciplinary approach to planning, implementation, and evaluation, which will include the effects of a number of factors that can affect its efficiency.

Some of the key terms related to computerized education merely include efficiency and effectiveness. These notions touch on the level and quality of learning outcomes, which are the generation of knowledge, skills, and habits. This goal cannot be achieved without efficient teaching work, which is again reflected in the ability to fulfill teaching objectives and tasks in a computerized environment. Without a doubt, the question of the quality and supremacy of machine learning is the issue that most of the science work in the area is currently focusing on. Coming from different scientific backgrounds, experts are trying to reach answers to questions about key factors and steps that lead to successful learning outcomes.

The effectiveness of machine learning, on the other hand, is largely viewed from the perspective of opportunities and support for students (interaction and instruction) in the adequate and accurate build-up of knowledge, skills, and habits through guided instruction and digital content. Any analysis of this and the previous questions inevitably leads to the consideration of all factors that influence the success of machine learning. To this end, a number of creators have focused their interest in studying various aspects of learning. These aspects include technological, psychological, financial, political, and many other influences that directly or indirectly affect machine learning, and therefore its outcomes.

To study the matter further, I've tried to discover and classify factors that impact the machine learning outcomes. I tried to answer the question:

What are the most important factors that affect the outcomes of machine learning?

I've decided to look into everything that might affect, contribute to, or limit, the outcomes of machine learning. The first thing I learned was that the learning outcomes largely depend on the program (software and curriculum design) itself and, but also teachers and students, or students, generally observed.

Many define the quality of machine learning to include learning outcomes, student experience, and the interface design. Unfortunately, in practice, it often comes to the fact that quality suffers from the speed of the program start-up.

Unlike traditional learning systems, machine learning opens up new questions and creates settings, in which technology serves as a foundation of both teaching and administrative activities. A new problem of pulling the boundaries between teaching and administration opens, which can make teachers' work more difficult and unclear.

The quality of machine learning is often viewed from the prospect of content and resources, although it essentially depends on the decisions and actions of those who participate in the process itself. Content quality should be viewed within the point of understanding the quality of machine learning, in the broadest of terms.

Machine learning takes place in a wide range of activities that technology completely pervades. The learning environment must be open and flexible, and it is, therefore, necessary to examine the key factors contributing to it.

Some of the factors known to contribute to successful machine learning are:

1. *Institutional support,* which includes the issues of technological infrastructure, technological plan and professional fees for faculties.

2. *The development of the courses*, which includes the development of the flow rate (courseware). The structure of

the course is mostly determined by the very schools or groups of faculty members.

3. *Teaching/learning process.* This category includes various educational and teaching activities, as well as modular learning, interactivity, and collaboration.

4. *Course structure.* This factor includes policies and procedures that affect the educational process, such as educational goals, the availability of literary resources, materials available to students, the time needed to answer students, and students' expectations.

5. *Support for students.* This category includes services that are normally encountered in student campuses, such as admission, financial assistance, training, and assistance to students in the use of the Internet.

7. *Evaluation and assessment* include policies and procedures governing the evaluation of the distance learning process.

Some of the key machine learning success factors include intellectual property, the construction of a computerized course, and the content of the computerized course, the computerized learning platform, the maintenance of a computerized course and the measurement of the success of the computerized course.

8. Technology, which includes ease of access and navigation, user interface design and level of interaction.

9. Teachers, his attitudes towards students, technical competences and interaction in the classroom and

10. The prior use of technology by the student and their previous knowledge.

11. The category of academic rigor includes course objectives and tasks, assignments to pupils, student participation, technology use, course content, and available resources.

12. The availability of the course, its structure, the use of images and graphics, the degree of interaction between students and the lecturer, as well as the type and quality of student work assessment.

Teacher's roles in digital learning

When studying machine learning and computerized learning environments as a whole, I note that the role of a teacher also receives a new form, and teachers themselves become guides, facilitators, leaders of the learning process, rather than "knowledge providers" they are in traditional classrooms. One of the main qualities of digital learning is the student's activity. The student has a 'main role' in the learning process. The teacher is there to navigate the process, balancing between the abundance of resources that a digital environment provides, and the student's needs. When I talk about student's 'needs', I see them as a broader subject than simply the need for knowledge. Students have their own unmeasurable capacities, talents, and interest. They have individual backgrounds and circumstances that shape their perceptions of the world. Students also need moral and emotional guidance, as well as opportunities to learn social skills from their teachers. In this sense, the teacher's role changed towards the following:

- Expertise in computerized teaching.
- The use of technology in teaching.

- Teacher training for ever-changing practices.

I'm simplifying a long list of complex teacher's roles here because the very essence of the matter isn't in the new tasks placed upon teachers. The essence of a transformation from a regular to a teacher of a digital classroom is in flexibility, adaptability to change, and recording and responding to the dynamics of an individual student and the entire class.

Student's qualities in the surroundings of digital learning

Unlike traditional student's role, that is more of a passive one, students in AI-guided learning surroundings face new requirements, such as:

Student readiness for computerized activity-technological skills, access to technology, technological literacy, self-directed learning (self-regulation); technological infrastructure - delivery system course, hardware and software, service provision;

Digital Content Requirements

Unlike traditional learning content, digital content too must undergo transformations to fit into the new surroundings. These are the requirements for digital learning content: provision of content and resources for learning - reusable learning objects; instructional design - reusable design of computerized course.

The student's relationship with the content

Placing students in the center of the learning process is precisely what defines learning as an active process in which a student communicates with his or her environment. A common subject of scientific interest is the study of student-content interaction, student-student, and student-teacher communication. As important factors, components of the learning environment, in particular, self-assessments, in which students evaluate themselves and seek feedback, play an important role in facilitating the learning process, and filling the gaps in knowledge.

The amount of time students spend on learning activities in the LMS shows that they first focused on content, evaluations, feedback, forum messages, and lastly, communication with the teacher. The content is an important component of the learning process and that it occupies the most attention of students. Content is one of the most important components of distant/computerized/AI education, although self-assessment tools also appear as an important component sparking the student's interest. This is a confirmation to designers and creators of computerized courses that these components are among the most important and that special attention should be paid to their design.

These factors play an important role in predicting students' achievements and can be influenced by the tools LMS uses in designing course and education. Students need the institution to assess their learning and their learning experiences. This should be taken into consideration in order to enable students to organize their own learning process.

Time and learning management

As a product of culture, communication tools are shaped by their social environment. CMC researchers have found that the use of communication technologies changes the linguistic culture. The way in which people communicate is largely shaped by the technology or media.

Inequality is present based on class affiliation in the form of individuals' ability to afford information communication technologies as well as the necessary skills needed to use many communication tools, such as writing emails, blogs and computerized forums. Infrastructural differences between rural and urban areas offer residents of urban areas better access to quality communication and technologies than rural residents.

Low-income households have less access to the Internet and have fewer personal computers than households with higher incomes and in urban areas. In countries lacking political stability, primary education for all children, and basic infrastructures such as clean water, housing, and electricity, which is often the case in countries with high rates of infectious curable diseases, infant mortality and malnutrition, can have a certain access to communication technologies such as mobile phone, but this does not apply to everyone and even to most citizens. Although technology can have global implications the reality of social circumstances can limit their impact.

Higher education, government, law, health, and other institutions offer an environment from which I can continue to explore the dynamics of human relationships and mechanical interfaces that influence and shape social meanings, interactions, production of knowledge and goods/services that societies produce and use.

AI-regulated learning environments

Machine Learning, AI, and machine learning

In scientific sources, the adjectives "virtual" and "computerized" are synonymous, in order to denote learning and education through the use of AI. The process of learning and education for acquiring qualifications not related to a traditional school institution is the subject of theoretical and practical studies in recent years, and the interest in this field is at its peak.

Machine learning is based on the link between dynamic knowledge management, learning, and training, as well as support for its realization, and its great importance is in creating opportunities and infrastructure for effective, specialized learning through e-courses. It depends on collecting and transforming relevant information into content that is appropriate to deliver to the learner at an appropriate time. When I mention machine learning, I also include open distance learning, Internet-based learning, and computer-based learning, technology-based learning and online learning as synonymous terms that that differ more in form than in essence.

Computerized learning is a form of education that takes place through the mediation of computerized media. Computerized media, in this case, play the role of intermediaries between teachers and students. This role is realized in the form of delivering learning materials, the role of the Internet as a means of communication, and a designed user interface as a learning environment, or "computerized classroom".

Machine learning tightly relates to learning through computerized media. Let's not forget that when designing an e-course we should also take into account educational and psychological knowledge and principles.

Instructional environment design

The design of instructional environments is based on theories of behaviorism, cognition, and constructivism, and technology-integrated into the educational process. Open Educational Practices are defined as the range of practices and links to the creation, use, and management of Open

Educational Resources. In a wider context, they signify a transition from learning based on resources to active learning in the process of social processes, reasoning, reflection, and innovation.

Machine learning environment

At present, the prevailing opinion is that existing machine learning environments do not conform to modern concepts of learning, and the trend of appreciating educational and psychological knowledge in compiling standard machine learning specifications is observed only relatively recently. A quality environment must not only provide conditions for successful learning but also has a high degree of usability. This environment must be adapted to different models of learning - constructivist learning, collaborative learning, experiential learning, and problem-based learning.

Taking into account the goal of learning is obligatory, in practice of computerized courses they are often reduced to the description, without collecting feedback on their achievements. Current machine learning systems do not offer adequate tools to measure the achievement of learning goals by students. The adaptability of the machine learning system can be enhanced with the possibility of creating a learning scenario. Examples of such systems are Moodle and PeU 2.0, which provides a smart computerized environment in which nonlinear learning scenarios can be developed.

It is important to consider three interrelated essential questions: the didactic structure of the course, methods and the planning of various educational activities. When it comes to choosing the right methods, they include lectures, discussions, interactive stimulation, problem-solving, design methods, exercises, assessment methods, and evaluation. These methods can be technologically advanced with different tools. The choice of an appropriate method depends on the form of education (distance learning or combined learning) and the type of learning (self-lectures, interactive stimulation, problem learning, exercises, learning scenarios defined by the author, or collaborative group work, project method, discussion;). Psychological characteristics of students: learning style that influences the choice of didactic methods.

The planning of educational activities includes the duration of learning specific modules, the duration of consultations of a face to face with tutors, schedules for assessing, sending tasks, and arranging discussions. There is a lack of content for machine learning, and most courses are in the field of information technology. There is a collective tendency to study the methodology and application of machine learning courses, the usability of these courses, the effectiveness of given courses, the use of adequate didactic terminology.

Principles of computerized Learning include principles: Sensory phenomena / pleasures: content must be receptive to multiple senses and have audio, graphics, animation, and video dimension

Personalized Learning: applications tailored to learner needs

With designing e-courses, there is a paradox in that, on the one hand, improving the quality of machine learning courses with sophisticated technological advancements, while at the same time denying the importance of setting educational goals. The methodology for the use of educational technologies is to credit for their rapid development, which is easy to understand, taking into account that the preparation and implementation of an educational experiments lasts at least six months. Psychological and educational machine learning theories also have great value in designing a machine learning environment that respects different learning styles. In that sense, it's worth pointing out that the framework through which one measures the effects of theories put into practice involves looking from the perspective of:

- Student-led learning: learning is driven by students determination through instructional materials and tests adapted to students' knowledge of the matter
- Meaningful measurement of student progress: simple questions addressed to the student through the course of the course in order to monitor his progress, as well as the measurement of learning outcomes
- Literary, humorous and relevant content: inclusion of games, role plays, simulations

Collecting, converting and delivering useful and accurate content that suits students' needs is of great importance. Computerized learning can take place in a synchronous and asynchronous forms. Synchronous computerized learning takes place in live contact within a virtual classroom, either through video contact or computerized communication. Asynchronous learning can take place at any time, the learner manages it independently, it is economically advantageous and components can be reused. It is more suitable for distant students.

In order to provide a uniform approach to the production and reuse of computerized learning components, a modular approach to computerized learning as well as building software, networks, and development basics are needed. In order to significantly improve machine learning procedures, seven essential standards have been identified: learning objects should be developed and reused, each authoring tool should have access to learning objects, learning objects should be stored within easy-access databases, streamlining the construction of courses through easy sequencing of content, and new granular assessment models.

Types of machine learning environments

Implementation of digital technologies into classrooms doesn't happen in a single form. The following are the different types of computerized environments:

Enhanced LMS, when interaction in computerized environments is enhanced using social networks, communication and content creation on Wiki, microblogging, Facebook.

Integrated LMS BYU OLN, COOPER - Collaborative Open Environment for Project Centered Learning, DIMPLE (Andone, 2011), eLearnTS, eMUSE, iCamp, Moodle, Google's Course Builder, and Open Source LMS, offering the possibility to host MOOCs, which integrates Google Social Media / collaborative educational tools.

Widgets Networks: integrate the specific and administrative features of social networks such as ROLE widgets that are integrated into Facebook and LinkedIn. These solutions could correspond to individual needs, but it is difficult to integrate continuous PLEs and communities of learning and practice of teachers and students.

Dedicated Networks: building specialized, dedicated social networks that provide hosting for virtual courses for courses: NeoLMS (formerly Edu2.0), LearnWorlds, attaCommunity (called the Facebook for learning), Edmodo or ProjectCampus.

The conceptual model for Open Learning Environments is based on educational technologies and theories that are developing with features that are educational, sociological and technological. This model can be used and verified by the work of research teams in including learning platforms based on different theories.

Inserting the computer into the classroom doesn't only change the look of the classroom, but also the entire teaching process.

AI and teaching

It's not difficult to note how a student benefits from learning in a personalized, digital environment versus traditional one; still, it takes looking into the broader framework of aspects that are relevant to the matter. The factors influencing the success of learning in the context of computerized education have for long been the subject of scientific work. From the perspective of pedagogy, psychology, technology, and even sociology and political science, numerous authors studied elements of computerized learning using a theoretical approach to the study, analysis of the evaluation of computerized probes. A significant number of studies were carried out using an experimental method.

Given the qualitative nature of the complex elements of computerized learning that unite humans and technology, many of them are largely subject to accurate and reliable statistical measurement.

Educational factors of AI learning

Educational factors, in most findings, include elements derived from teachers themselves from one instruction and on the other, as well as content factors.

Teacher factors include elements such as interaction with students, feedback, academic qualifications and professional development.

The instructional design factors refer to elements such as cooperation and teamwork, engaging higher levels of cognitive structure of students, equality and diversity of learning resources, learning materials, active learning, learning activities, student motivation, design standards, evaluation, use of graphics and media, attractiveness of students, data rate and inclusiveness.

Content factors include elements such as the accuracy and relevance of the content, the content of the content, the renewal and improvement of the content.

Teacher Factors.

Corrective feedback. Teachers emphasize that adequate, timely and concise feedback focused on knowledge correction is one of the most important factors influencing the achievement of students in computerized education programs. Teachers also constantly monitor the understanding of content by students to identify possible gaps in knowledge and understanding of content and help students solve dilemmas that may arise from insufficient or misunderstandings of content.

Analyzing the results of a good practice, it's worth pointing out that teachers emphasize the importance of taking care of the personal circumstances of the course participants. They use surveillance as a method of identifying students who are in any personal crisis or problem, and especially if it is a problem related to learning. While there's an abundance of sources that help students to overcome personal crises, what is lacking are professional materials that deal with this problem in the context of a machine learning environment.

Interaction with students. What defines learning as an active process in which a student communicates with his environment is placing students at the center of the learning process. Studying student-content interaction, pupil-student and student-teacher is often the subject of scientific interest, and important components of the impact on communication are the components of the learning environment, in particular the self-assessment component, in which students can assess themselves and receive feedback on their own knowledge, learning and results.

These factors have an important impact on the educational process, and monitoring these factors can help fill gaps in learning and knowledge. Below, I will analyze and highlight the characteristics and specificities of some of the key elements outside the officially prescribed curriculum that affect learners within the computerized environment.

Elements of non-verbal communication, such as facial expressions, mimics, body language, and speech tone are an important factor in understanding the connotative meaning of messages that are communicated among class participants. If these elements are missing, communication is deprived of emotional and affective meaning. Also, when the form of communication is deprived of non-verbal elements, errors in the interpretation of messages are possible, which can lead to confusion in the conversation. The very lack of emotional and affective elements of communication can negatively affect the motivation for learning and work. In computerized communication, it is difficult to set up a signature and provide illustrations and examples related to the topic being discussed.

Computerized communication also has a more formal tone than direct communication, so many elements of spontaneous communication are lost which enables further clarification of misunderstandings. These disadvantages in computerized education are first reflected in problems of understanding computerized messages and instructions given within the user interface. Misunderstanding or incomprehensible understanding of given instructions makes the work of course participants more difficult, which adversely affects their motivation for work and leads to poorer results of the work involved.

The role of teachers is emphasized in the environment of computerized learning, in particular, its intermediary and coordinating position. The use of ICT allows the teacher to use a more effective and more impressive presentation of learning materials, which drastically changes the traditional audiovisual environment of the lesson. In order to prevent obstacles in successful communication that could negatively affect the learning process, teachers use multiple specific tactics.

In order to respond to new learning requirements, the teacher must develop a new perception and attitude towards an instructive approach and his own role in the instructional process, which should transform him into an e-teacher.

New teacher demands relate to the knowledge of the use of word processors, the addition and modification within the software, surfing the Internet, the use of e-mail, discovering connections, and providing support to students, stimulating students' interest in the matter and learning about learning strategies in a new, computerized environment. More precisely, one of the most important roles of teachers is to teach students how to learn.

Inside an e-classroom, the teacher is a student's leader, a mentor, and a facilitator in the use of technologies for the purpose of supplying and organizing information, problem-solving, and providing administrative support in the form of describing the process, recording student progress and activities, leading students to conclusions, and referring them to adequate literature references. The teacher's task is also to initiate activity among students who will mediate in successful learning as well as the ability to adequately assess student progress using funds dictated by a planned computerized protocol.

All teaching methods and techniques should be combined into a harmonious whole, and the combination of instructive methods should include tasks and activities that learners will perform independently, in small groups or in the entire class. When it comes to the application of ICT, the teacher should always keep in mind possible improvements. In general, the teacher should have a built awareness of the meaning and importance of key terms related to machine learning, and in particular, combine the competencies he possesses as an expert in machine learning process that is yet to be created.

Communication with students. The dialectic relationship that exists between individual and social systems results in successful socialization and the integration of socially approved norms, values, and beliefs. As a product of culture, communication tools are shaped by their social environment. The use of communication technologies changes the linguistic culture, as the way in which I communicate is largely shaped by the technology or media use. This leads to a focus on changes in social interactions and an increase in technology environments.

By analyzing students' emotions, potential problems can be anticipated within the course. Since the techniques for detecting emotions should be as least intrusive as possible so as not to endanger the work of students, researchers suggest analyzing student's activities as the least intrusive technique. Another possibility is the analysis of written work and information that students leave to get information about their emotions.

Teachers are now able to detect emotions from the student's essays and use the dimension of anger as a measure of motivation. There was a strong correlation found between the level of anger that was detected in the essays and the student's interest in studying the subject.

Teachers emphasize the importance of caring for the personal circumstances of the course participants. They use surveillance as a method of identifying students who are in any personal crisis or problem, and especially if it is a problem related to learning.

Professional development. Teacher's attitude, values, beliefs, and perceptions inevitably affect the attitude of teachers toward students. This theoretical "heritage" of teachers has a decisive role in the way in which they look at the student, their place and role in the education process, and directly in the classroom, as well as the process of education itself.

Some of the ways for teachers to respond to the invisible influence of the implicit curriculum are their personal characteristics, professional ethics, and educational competencies through the values of lifelong learning and professional development.

With different forms of computerized communication, such as discussions, forums, e-mails, there is a specific sense of mental distance from the person with whom the participant communicates. This can have both a positive and a negative impact, and in the context of 'teachers and pupils' relationships, it can make it easier for students to communicate with teachers without the fear of authority. This kind of communication with teachers is often more pleasant to students than direct contact, especially because feedback, instructions, or explanations that a student receives from a document are permanently recorded for future needs. Computerized communication also allows students to communicate their thoughts more clearly and concisely as a result of the absence of fear of authority.

In computerized education systems, timelines and limitations are precisely defined. Also, a lot of effort is invested in the objectivity and precision of feedback that students receive. Time frames for providing feedback in the computerized environment are arranged in such a way to provide timely information, therefore, there are deadlines within which a student will receive an answer to a question or an assessment of his / her work. On the other hand, testing and examinations within computerized education programs are often pre-programmed, so the student gets feedback on their success immediately after the completion of the test.

In order to respond to qualitatively different requirements of machine learning, the teacher's task is to develop a new perception and attitude towards an instructive approach and its own role in the instructional process, which should transform them into an e-teacher.

AI: Student's benefits

Cooperation and teamwork

In an effort to maintain the presence of the academic spirit within the virtual environment of computerized teaching, teachers use regular monitoring and keep the students aware that they are being noticed, pointing out the importance of respecting the general terms and norms of the program. Using previously mentioned communication principals, teachers regularly remind students to respect school norms, whether it is to prevent cheating and other disciplinary violations or to interact students in forums and discussion boards.

Effective learning involves the multiple functions of different systems organized into reciprocal spirals, with multiple instruction systems dependent on the design of the instruction, including the interaction of students with a teacher and student with content. Learning largely depends on self-regulation and self-medication or mediation through another agent. There's a notable lack of metacognitive awareness of one's own learning in institutional school education, which begs pointing out that the learning process is more effective in environments where individuals within the group direct their own learning and the learning and learning of other members.

Asynchronous computerized learning can positively influence the achievement of an effective higher-order learning through a rich cognitive presence. Higher-order learning is reflected in the dimensions of reflection, self-management, and metacognition. By asynchronous learning, I mean the possibility of a collaborative learning within the frames of a personalized environment for an individual, in a way that guarantees equal interaction and independence from the group. This possibility did not exist in earlier forms of learning and distinguishes a synchronism and connectivity as key features of computerized learning.

The metacognitive awareness of faculty students in some findings I came across showed a weaker ability to predict learning outcomes and educational scenarios using dual encoding strategies, static presentations, representing uninteresting information, testing, and separation. Better learning outcomes and more accurate possibilities for assessment were demonstrated among students who received targeted instruction and those students who were directly exposed to those assessments from which the results were obtained. This suggests that college students are largely unconscious of strategies that could help them memorize course information. It has been found that training in memory strategies has potential opportunities to improve metacognitive abilities in these areas.

Since attendees of computerized courses rely heavily on instruction in learning, they may lose the ability to self-regulate. The lack of self-regulation in learning can lead to academic failure, while good self-regulators can control their own cognition, motivation, and behavior in order to achieve their own goals. It is very important for the educational practice to build effective computerized environments for self-regulation, which should contribute to the creation of friendly environments for machine learning, such as discussion boards and homework, in order to enhance students' motivation, in particular, the interior motivation that affects satisfaction. In order to make students more aware of the usefulness and satisfaction of computerized learning, it is important to encourage their self-efficacy. The observed usefulness of machine learning is growing with the growing appeal of the environment.

Quality of computerized learning

As computerized learning creates new contexts, constraints and raises many questions, it is fundamentally different from traditional learning. Technology has significantly affected many of the functions within the schools and universities, such as administration, behavior, and teaching. In this respect, quality is seen from the perspective of course design, contextual student experience, and learning outcomes. The quality of machine learning is also viewed through content or resources and is also conditioned and dependent on the decisions and behaviors of practitioners and participants in an computerized course. The quality of resources is ensured through shaping and leading a quality learning process. Let's not forget that the same quality criteria related to the process of computerized education and learning apply to the process of education and learning in general.

Troubleshooting

The importance of the "development of the solution" activity proves the importance of developing a common solution space for collaborative tasks. The importance of managing the interaction process is in the fact that the training course has had a role in an environment that required more coordination than face-to-face contact. It has been proven that activities focused specifically on content and coordination define activities in a collaborative process. Learning outcomes are more complex and indicate the importance of collaborative problem-solving activities in distinguishing successful from unsuccessful groups.

Factors that influence the efficiency of machine learning are: learning at the individual pace, greater interactivity with the student, understanding improved graphics presentation, greater relevance of content, efficiency and comfort of students, faster passage through the course because teaching can simultaneously be provided to a massive number of users across the globe.

Motivation

Learning through the Internet and within PLE's can have a positive impact on student motivation. These influences stem from the precise and concise nature of computerized communications, which enables timely information and feedback.

The demands placed on the students are clearly and precisely defined, eliminating the possibility of misinterpreting the instructions. Students who attend the course receive guidance, tests, and instructions for completing them, including a transparent assessment system, where they are clearly informed of what is expected of them and what they must do to achieve a satisfactory result.

Computerized education systems, in most cases, leave a positive impression on students. Students then form positive attitudes and expectations towards e-education in general, which improves their motivation to join in some future forms of computerized education.

Self-regulation

Machine learning satisfaction can be predicted based on interactive learning environments, self-efficacy and displayed anxiety. Interactive learning environments and perceptions of self-efficacy in computerized learning can be affected by the perceived utility of the course. Satisfaction with computerized learning contributes to the usefulness of machine learning.

It is very important for the practice to build effective computerized environments for self-regulation, which should contribute to the creation of friendly environments for machine learning, such as discussion boards and homework, in order to enhance students' motivation, in particular, interior motivation affects satisfaction while external influences on utility. In order to make students more aware of the usefulness and satisfaction of computerized learning, it is important to encourage their self-efficacy. Students' attitudes towards machine learning systems can be divided into three groups. In the first group, individual characteristics and quality of the System can affect effective and cognitive spheres, while cognitive and affective groups can influence groups of behavioral intentions. Affective and cognitive spheres are associated with noticeable utility and pleasure, while the behavioral component contains an observable self-regulation.

Four factors should be considered when developing the computerized Learning Systems: individual characteristics of students, useful characteristics of the environment, positive attitudes of students and effective learning activity. The learning activity can be influenced by the characteristics of the environment, the satisfaction of the environment in the form of observed satisfaction and usefulness and learning characteristics in the form of observed self-efficacy.

Fast, timely and concise feedback

In computerized education systems, timelines and limitations are precisely defined. Also, a lot of effort is invested in the objectivity and precision of feedback that students receive as soon as possible. Time frames for providing feedback in the computerized environment are arranged in such a way to provide timely information, therefore, there are deadlines within which a student will receive an answer to a question or an assessment of his / her work. On the other hand, testing and examinations within computerized education programs are often pre-programmed, so the student gets feedback on his success immediately after the completion of the test.

Equal opportunities for the participation of students of different cultural and social milieu or environment

Only computer and internet access are required to participate in e-education programs. Given the more affordable prices of the program, students with lower incomes can afford it, and given that e-education does not require a change of place of residence and additional costs, it provides equal opportunities for students from different cultural and social backgrounds to study under equal conditions. Under such conditions, students are willing to communicate with participants from different countries, cultures and different social status. The mutual exchange of opinions and experiences among students helps them to enrich their knowledge and broader aspects. In this way, students who come from economically and socially marginalized environments can expand their aspects of knowledge that their local environment cannot provide. On the other hand, students who come from environments with a high standard of living can learn a lot about the real problems that their peers from other parts of the world encounter.

Interaction

Interaction, along with the concept of communication, is one of the key concepts of educational science. Educational-educational process, education and education in their comprehensiveness are conditioned by interaction and communication. The educational process, as a subject of the study of educational science, is essentially composed of sending and receiving messages among individuals.

In this section, I have opted for this view of the concept of communication, taking into account the fact that for learning success through computerized educational programs, which is, to some degree, the ultimate purpose and goal of each computerized educational brochure, and at the same time the collective goal of the participants in the educational process in In this sense, the crucial interpretation of messages, in the form of instructions and feedback.

In this section, I will look at the importance of feedback in the communication process, considering the fact that feedback is one of the key factors in the effectiveness of interaction and communication in the machine learning process.

Communication

This definition of communication, of a very broad scope, is adequate to the context of our work and the problem I are studying, because it sets a broad and flexible framework for understanding communication within the computerized environment, which offers wide opportunities for simultaneous communication between individuals and groups.

The communication process in contemporary education includes all elements of a didactic quadrilateral: teachers, students, content exchanged and educational technology - that is, communication channels or media. Communication in education has two basic content components: (1) information-cognitive component and (2) social-emotional component. A student has certain intellectual needs, hence receives and interprets both categories of information, and then reacts to them and sends such information to others. The communication process is the basis and foundation of the educational process. Successful communication is based on and depends on every educational effort and effort. When discussing computerized communication from the perspective of computerized learning, efficiency and machine learning results depend on its effectiveness. For this reason, I consider the features of communication in the machine learning process is of great importance for a better understanding of the learning process within the computerized environment.

Communication with other students

Man, as a social being, naturally seeks to establish contacts and associate with other people for the purpose of working together and achieving the goal. Learning is, in addition to the individual and social process, a process in which students exchange impressions, information and explanations with their peers. When the student is isolated from the group, and if the educational program does not offer the possibility of group work and mutual counseling, interest and motivation for learning can degrade.

The competitive spirit and the need for students to compare each other in order to build a picture of their own position in relation to others are highly expressed in traditional higher education. Most computerized education programs do not provide this possibility, which can affect students' motivation and their need for achievement. The authority of the experts under whose mentorship is taught, that is, faith and respect for that person are significantly influenced by the amount of effort that students will invest in learning. Learning in a digitally designed environment, a student can feel alone, isolated, in the absence of interaction with other program participants, which is another factor that can have a negative impact.

I classify the basic tasks of any form of teaching as material, educational, and functional. Educational, ie material teaching tasks, relate to acquiring, acquainting, understanding and applying knowledge as well as forming concepts. The task of teaching is to develop intellectual, practical, psychomotor, verbal and other abilities in students. Under the educational tasks of teaching I mean the formation and adoption of moral, aesthetic, physical, work and other values.

Justifiably, I ask myself: "Can computerized learning accomplish all three key teaching tasks equally, or better, than the traditional classroom?" Can the machine learning environment contribute to achieving educational and functional teaching tasks as well as the material teaching goals?

One of the ways in which experts pay attention to this question is through analyzing collaborative learning and learning through problem-solving in computerized teaching surroundings. Let's look into one important question: Whether and how does collaborative learning and learning through problem-solving differ in virtual and real learning environments? In order to answer this question, I focused on studying problem-solving in virtual learning environments and classroom teaching.

Some of the outcomes I came across measured though follow-up of activities with virtual groups showed the same effects in a group that was taught digitally and groups taught in face-to-face teaching.

The importance of the "solution development" activity is the importance of developing a common solution space for collaborative tasks. The importance of managing the interaction process displays in the fact that the professional training course had a role in an environment that required more coordination in relation to face-to-face instruction.

Activities focused specifically on content and coordination define activities in a collaborative process. Learning results are more heterogeneous for complex real cases and indicate the importance of collaborative problem-solving activities in distinguishing successful from unsuccessful groups.

The effectiveness of eLearning is largely viewed from the viewpoint of opportunities and support for learners in the adequate and accurate build-up of knowledge, skills, and habits through guided instruction and didactically shaped, digital content. Any review of this and the previous questions inevitably leads to the consideration of all factors that influence the success of machine learning. Aspects involving technological, educational, psychological, financial, political and other influences condition the success of acquiring knowledge digitally.

In order to deepen our study and emphasize the importance of many factors, I analyzed AI-based elements in the light of the all aspects that are otherwise important to evaluate the learning outcomes.

In order to answer this question, I tried to determine the general grounds of computerized education and learning and group the discovered factors of action to the success of computerized learning in a logical system.

First, I looked at the different theoretical basis, involving multiple theories of learning that were used to lay the very foundation of any course, including computerized learning. As the broadest theoretical framework, these concepts emphasize informal education. Informal education is the result of the application of different educational and learning theories and is sparked by technological progress and the development of educational technologies.

The constructivist theory of learning is the theoretical framework and the prospective influence of this review, as it is most scientifically confirmed and methodologically advanced. Constructivism recognizes the previous knowledge and understanding with which participants enter the learning situation. Learning comes in the active learning and integration of newly acquired and previous knowledge and experience.

Analyzing the fundamentals and the development of non-formal education inevitably leads to the study of learning theories that emphasize students' activity in acquiring knowledge and experience, such as constructivist learning theory, theory of experiential learning, situational, active and relational learning.

The theory of connectionism is often viewed as the basis for the development of informal education. The theory of connectionism, which emphasizes the connection of people and science beyond the geographical constraints and phenomenon of globalization, as a process that follows, highlights and uses the development of science, acknowledging that globalization shapes the reality by connecting individuals, groups and communities through scientific and technological achievements. The theory of connectionism seeks to affirm the positive aspects of such scientific and technological progress.

Analyzing the theoretical roots of computerized education, I have established that it, historically, was derived from the initial forms of distance education. Transmitted by the development of information and communication technologies, distance education has evolved into a form of education that is difficult to classify exclusively in any form of education (formal, informal, informal). Observed from the point of application, computerized education is present in all three essential forms of education. In this section, I have chosen to look at it in the context of informal education, because it is a side that provides an understanding of the term from a multi-dimensional aspect and with the least constraints. From the perspective of non-formal education, computerized education has the widest meaning.

According to the many, definitions of computerized education, its basic qualities are independence and media mediation (ICT). From here, computerized education can involve independent research through information and communication technologies, as well as attending a computerized course in order to improve the acquired professional skills. The main qualities of computerized education emphasize its availability, universality, flexibility, based on the premises of equal right of everyone to lifelong learning and learning.

Machine learning is a term that is defined by similar terms, with the differences that relate to the learning process. Machine learning is a process that is mediated by information technology, independent of time and environment, universally accessible to those individuals who have access to the Internet. As a phenomenon, it is a frequent subject of scientific research.

The study of the phenomenon of computerized learning throws light on the qualitative nature of the process, revealing its conditionality by students' activity, the basis on various forms of active learning (experimental, situational, relational, programmed, etc.), as well as a multitude of factors, that is, verifiable, what determines the effectiveness and learning outcomes.

AI Overcomes Cheating and Plagiarism

During the period of intense development of computerized education and learning by using computerized sources, the Internet was viewed as a medium through which students can access numerous and non-censored sources of knowledge. In this setting, the Internet is viewed as a source of unlimited knowledge and information, which is now offered to a large number of average students on a "silver plate". The availability of educational content through the use of educational technology in the last decades has significantly increased, and in the present time, the average student in a number of virtual steps has access to exhaustive databases of theoretical and research character.

With the affirmation of learning digitally, but also "machine learning," as one of the hybrid forms of education that slowly but surely leaves most of the established classifications of education programs and systems, there's an increase in recorded improvements and benefits in the quality of learning, work and personal development of students. There are also fears of the adverse impact of this kind of learning on the development of students in general, including his physical as well as moral, intellectual, spiritual, aesthetic and development of working skills.

With the growing scientific interest in this field, numerous repeated researches have established, now well-known, negative consequences that the computerized environment can have on the process of learning and the development of students as individuals. Researchers criticize the way in which information comes from, the criteria for selecting relevant information and legitimate sources against the source and information of doubtful origin and quality, but also the way in which the computerized environment "educates" the personality of the student during the time of intense development, whether I are talking about a pupil of elementary school age or a university student.

Nowadays many times repeated, expanded and exhaustive research has revealed a worrying rise in the manifestation and presence of morally undesirable forms of behavior and personality traits in the computerized environment. Researchers find that many of the key moral values, such as respect and truth, are threatened in the computerized environment. Researchers often find themselves caught in the lack of elements of moral and legal sanctions for immoral behavior, as well as the design of a computerized environment that gives the user many rights and benefits without expecting responsibility for their own behavior.

The increase in the number of academic fraud cases and the general decline in the ethics of moral behavior in computerized learning communities, but also generally in the use of computerized sources has been noticeable since the late 1980s and has been worryingly growing over decades. According to recent findings, not only a growing number of students resort to some form of scam over the Internet, but they also do not recognize the meaning and consequences of their work, and in many cases, they do not even consider them to be wrong.

The problem of the ethics of behavior, academic fraud and plagiarism attracted my interest and drove me to explore it within the current educational reality. A significant number of carefully designed research gave results that support the thesis of the problem of ethics of behavior in computerized environments: the frequency of many forms of cheating, the negative consequences on the learning process in the form of non-criticality and superficiality in the study of computerized sources, to forms of aggressive and criminal behavior on the Internet, such as computerized bullying (cyberbullying) and violation of other's privacy. However, alarming "signals" on moral behavior on the Internet do not appear only in the results of scientific research.

Unfortunately, a highly profitable market for the production and plagiarisation of intellectual content, in the form of a tremendous number of websites around the world trading with the writing and selling of academic sections, essays, and studies on all levels of education, in my mind speak in favor of moral as well as intellectual decline in the values of education. This highly profitable and well-networked market charges high for its "products", and ensures the legality of its own work by waving the responsibility for the use of content and by voluntarily renouncing the original authors of their rights in exchange for material compensation. With the insight that, with a sufficient amount of paid money, an individual can provide himself with copyright on the content in which he did not even participate, and which provides him with academic prestige on (worryingly) all academic levels, from basic to doctorate, inspired me to study this problem further.

In this chapter, I will examine the problem of plagiarism and academic fraud by investigating the important causes, indications, and strategies for preventing such unethical practices in education. Here, I will try to answer the questions: What are the characteristics, changes, and concerns registered in the ethics of students' behavior on the

Internet in the context of learning by using computerized sources and participating in e-education programs? What are the causes of academic fraud and plagiarism in a computerized environment? What are the strategies for improving the ethics of student behavior and the fight against academic fraud in order to improve the ethics of pupil behavior, enrichment, and enhancement of the quality of learning through computerized media and the moral growth of students in general? Through searching for answers to these questions, the aim of this chapter will be to offer a systematic and concise overview of the key points of the problem, with an emphasis on the strategies for its resolution.

Moral and Learning

The process of moral education itself arises in the unity of the objective and subjective aspects of moral education. While the external side of moral education expresses the demands of society, the personal side of moral education refers to character building by social norms and laws, as well as the relation of personality to other people and society. Since the main task of education is to transform external moral requirements into the individual norms of personal behavior, the logical path of moral development as a process is reflected in the adoption of knowledge on the basis of which an individual forms their own system of moral values, develops their own moral experience and moral feelings.

In order to gain knowledge of moral norms into forms of moral perfection, the space between these two categories must be filled with practice, a relationship of experience in which the individual is in a position to make moral decisions and resolve moral dilemmas. The necessities for this are moral needs, which are generated by the formation of a system of conviction and moral sentiment. A holistic, moral personality can only be formed by the unification of these two sides.

In this section, I will study how the virtual environment influences the formation of willing and characteristic features in students, as well as its impact on the appearance of undesirable forms of moral behavior and negative character traits.

Plagiarism

Plagiarism violates the intellectual property rights of the original author, regardless of the amount and degree of plagiarism committed. With adequate guidance and quotation, the use of other intellectual property is permitted without the permission of the author. However, plagiarism is also considered in cases where credit is not given to the author in an adequate way.

There are several types of plagiarism. The first form is a direct download (so-called "copy") of another's content, and the other is simply paraphrasing, or the use of other content without significant change, except for replacing a certain number of words with synonyms.

Here, I ask the question: Are there any additional forms of plagiarism that are not yet defined by legal regulations, and can paraphrasing, which requires only so much engagement to avoid plagiarism, be considered as legitimate intellectual work? Is this type of work, although not in itself a plagiarism, accepted as an ethically acceptable form of behavior and a legitimate academic contribution?

In computerized communities, especially blogs and forums dealing with plagiarism, users often share information that can help recognize skillfully plagiarized content. Within these communities, plagiarism by translating (use of content by a simple translation into another language) and so-called "rewriting" (minimal change of text to "deceive" computerized detectors of plagiarism and its restructuring). This form of plagiarism by rewriting differs from simple paraphrasing in that it involves the use of a larger number of synonyms of the original content so that plagiarism cannot be proven by testing with computerized detectors, nor by observation.

Moral behavior in a computerized environment

In this chapter, I ask the question: Does computerized education, driven by the principle of availability, equity, and multiculturalism, have in its design also the limitations of ethical nature that jeopardize its most important characteristic, the quality of education? The quality of education that any educational institution provides is closely related to the legitimacy, ethics, professionalism, or the lack of the above, in its work. Through the analysis of the ethical dimensions, I will try to deliver the ethical framework of computerized education and point to the "burning" issues in this context, that is, the alarming phenomena to which attention should be paid.

The philosophy of education has shifted so that emphasis is put on the cognitive sphere and preparation for the efficient performance of the functions necessary on the market, while the education of the total personality and all of its components are neglected.

The utilitarian appreciation of learning, in which an individual prepares exclusively for a professional role, is also narrowly leading to the education of a personality that is one-dimensional. Such a person is trained to do exclusively well for themselves and the market.

I advocate the importance of a harmonious, harmonious view of mankind from all social and individual aspects. I believe that social reality must be respected equally in the theoretical and practical activities, as well as the individual characteristics of the educator and their personal development. The theory of moral education forms policies and rules, which represent the most general requirements for moral behavior. The norms arising from the rules based on laws represent the illustration of moral principles. The best way to accept moral norms is precisely the real-world experience.

I discovered a set of six ethical principles that can guide the computerized education. These principles include competence, integrity, professionalism, social and scientific responsibility, respect for the rights and dignity of individuals and the care of the welfare of others. I see many possibilities for the computerized education to contribute to the building of cultural, social and academic values, as well as to really contribute to the social equality of students, regardless of their diversity. To tackle this topic, it's important for one to be aware of dilemmas related to computerized education, like equality in education vs. digital self, ethical dilemmas of multiculturalism, ethics of participation, commitments, ethics of automation, control and privacy, identity, confidentiality of data and anonymity, psychological distance and academic fraud, and the quality of computerized education.

These dilemmas relate to serious, crucial issues of computerized education, such as quality, social equity and multiculturalism, data security, but also to copyright safety.

The first difficulty to overcome is the contradiction of the idea of equality in computerized education, in contrast to the digital self that, in this case, shows the lack of direct interaction among the participants. Despite the wide availability and flexibility of computerized education, it's too early to speak about its universal availability. The availability of the Internet and information technology is not universal, but the class privilege remains.

Multiculturalism, as the principle on which the modern concept on which the education is based in general, including computerized education, provides an opportunity for members of different cultures to equally participate in education. However, there's a risk of misunderstandings in interaction and communication, which come precisely due to the differences between cultures. In the context of multiculturalism. The importance of the learning culture being formed in the process of teaching is grand, and it should influence the behavior of students outside the classroom. It points to the responsibility of the educational institution for the ethics of student behavior and the necessity of training teachers to work in a multicultural classroom.

The dimension of the obligation to participate is another trait of computerized education. A student is required to attend certain actions at a given time, including discussions. The issue of the ethics of this aspect of machine learning is raised, that is (un)ethical to create a necessity for the student to participate in discussions that beyond his or hers abilities and interests.

Automation is a process characterized by trends in the development of modern technology, including information and communication technologies, which greatly affect education. In the setting of computerized education, automation occurs in the process of transferring knowledge, delivering information, providing feedback, and evaluating student work. The legitimacy of assessment here is also in question, as it is based on an automated process, therefore the namely assuring quality of the acquired.

By using the computerized education system, all individuals involved provide companies and organizations with an abundance of information about their personality, actions, knowledge, and proper behavior on the Internet. Such data is nowadays commercialized, and companies use them for the purpose of customizing their own products with the wants and needs of users. The issue of ethics in the use of personal data collected in this way is raised, especially considering the fact that the involved in computerized education do not have the possibility to control this process, and most often they are not aware of it.

The ethical dilemma that interests me the most is the phenomenon of psychological distance and academic fraud. Unfortunately, as many as 59% of participants in computerized education admit that they have committed some form of academic fraud. Regarding the quality of education that e-courses and universities should provide, this devastating figure indicates the seriousness of the issue of academic fraud and the validity of competencies acquired through computerized education. Some explanations of this problem relate to the phenomenon of a psychological distance, that is, the possibility of computerized education, to facilitate students forming those attitudes and values that lead to ethical behavior.

Academic integrity is the contribution of each individual and a way for them to be recognized and respected. Academic work is based on the expectations of civilized behavior, credibility, and honesty. Educators have a duty to cultivate academic integrity standards in all educational activities.

There's a connection of talent and moral behavior among students in the context of computerized education. Here, I point out to three groups of theories of intelligence: Gardner's Multiple Intelligence Theory, which includes linguistic, logical, mathematical, spatial, music, naturalistic, interpersonal and intrapersonal potential, which includes moral evaluation; theories that represent the view that an individual is born with a certain moral concept that develops through maturation, such as Kolberg, Grin, Haidt, Hauser, and others; Natural intelligence highly correlates with moral behavior. Children with higher intelligence pay more attention to moral issues, concern for the needs and feelings of others, and they are more interested in ethical issues. As particularly important forms of intelligence, logical, mathematical and interpersonal intelligence are the forms that include understanding and consideration of attitudes, beliefs, needs, thoughts, and feelings of others. For a gifted individual, computerized learning involves participation, creativity, and connectivity.

The problem of plagiarism in computerized education indicates the alarming occurrence of plagiarism and various forms of academic fraud in student work, highlighting scientifically collected data from the 1996-1998 period, according to which between 3 and 13% make some form of academic scam in his work. However, you still need to look at this percentage with some reserve, since the research was based on the self-assessment of the students. Compared to three surveys conducted between 1988 and 2004, there's an increase in the percentage of plagiarism among students. In one, 3% of students saw plagiarism by copying content and simply paraphrasing previously submitted student sections, while other identified plagiarism by copying and simple paraphrasing from computerized sources in 13% of respondents. This percentage is rising in 2004 with detected plagiarism by copying and simply paraphrasing all available sources in 21% of students. The percentage continues to grow, which you can see from the showing that 28% of students at least once plagiarized the content.

Using the manual method, teachers were able to detect plagiarism was in 2.8% of adult students, while the automatic method detected plagiarism in 12.8% of students. The percentage of self-leveled plagiarism by students is significantly higher in the percentage compared to that observed by external testing. This can lead us to re-examine the power of the software to fully detect plagued content, but also to examine students' perceptions of specific procedures they consider plagiarism.

Causes of academic fraud and plagiarism in computerized education

The main features of learning by using computerized media, which can have equally positive and negative effects on the learning and behavior of students relate to the skill of performing multiple tasks at the same time, learning by searching for information and their current profitability and a wide range of attention to learning outcomes.

As the negative effects of the speed of data transmission in learning by using computerized sources is an intolerance to waiting for answers or feedback while performing multiple tasks at the same time has negative neurological effects on the concentration of attention and the depth of the processing of information related to the material being taught. Other data shows that learning by doing multiple activities simultaneously requires more time and is significantly less effective, which points to changes in learning modes in younger generations of learning that are becoming more and more difficult to concentrate on the idea they are currently studying and they look deeper.

Learning by searching for information and its current profitability, leads to superficial learning based on short and shallow "scanning", in addition to "skimming" the studied texts in order to find the necessary materials as quickly and efficiently as possible. In this process, students tend to identify sources that contain the most keywords related to the subject they study, not paying attention to the relevance of the specific content and the legitimacy of its source.

Taking into account the results of multiple research in this field of interest, I've compiled a list of the effects of these characteristics on learning outcomes. Impatience and lack of perseverance, focus, chronic superficiality and the formation of physical and mental laziness are the main negative effects of learning in a computerized environment that offers "quick and easy" access to educational materials. Learning is a process that requires patience and perseverance in efforts to discover and study relevant sources, however, in a virtual space that offers access to large amounts of data without obstacles, it turns out that students are less willing to invest in searching for relevant materials. Instead, there is circulation with less relevant materials if they are easier to access. Focusing on studying a particular topic, either by self-study or listening to lectures, accounts for a wide span of attention. The formation of a wide span of attention comes precisely through doing multiple activities at the same time.

In the context of learning outcomes, a wide range of attention negatively affects the depth of learning, affecting the quality of the process itself. By skimming a vast number of computerized pages, students are used to superficial reading, with insufficient attention to the reading material. By directing their attention to key phrases and words within the text, students are inclined to pay attention only to the smaller parts of the text that seem to contain the largest amount of requested words. This shallowness makes it difficult for students to study matter deeply when necessary. This practice of learning leads to the formation of physical and mental laziness. Understandably, the hours spent in front of the monitor for activities that should represent learning or studying, and in fact reduced to the superficial flyover of huge amounts of published material, does not provoke legitimacy, and acceptance and adoption of a small percentage of the text based on the keyword and phrase contained, leads to physical and mental laziness.

Always looking for an easier and faster path, students become frustrated when they encounter obstacles or fail in their intention to reach the "appropriate" sources in a short period of time. These students easily give up their work and turn to repeating well-trained strategies, although they do not have to be the right fit for the topic or the subject. Recalling the context of the ethics of students' behavior in computerized environments, which is the perspective of this section, it is not difficult for one to see the possible effect of these factors on turning students into violators of moral but also written copyright laws. I believe that the need for faster and easiest information retrieval, along with their shallow and non-critical view, combined with non-tolerance of frustration among students, can certainly influence their decision to go through "lesser resistance" and to mislead the misuse of someone else's intellectual property. Non-sensitivity of the net-generation leads to moral issues, the frequency of lying, causing harm and pain to others, destruction of relationships, theft, etc. Therefore, the need to draw attention to the new wave of youth behavior in the virtual world and the impact on educational qualities, especially the development of (non) self-criticism and respect for oneself and respect for others.

Consequences of unethical behavior in education on personal and professional development and community

In order to look at the wide range of effects that the culture of unethical behavior on the Internet has on the development of the individual and the implications that the evolving machine learning culture has on the development of individuals and communities, I looked at views on the moral development of an individual. The field of social and moral education and behavior is very complex. A whole series of factors are involved in the behavior of individuals and groups. Moral understanding is conditioned by general social values, tradition, culture, education, and so on.

The complexity of social and moral development consists in the fact that a complex process involves a number of different factors. In the moral perceptions of the individual, in addition to upbringing, culture, tradition, and general social values are also reduced. The complexity of moral development stems from the individual's individuality, and along with its conditionality, by many factors. Since moral development takes place within the framework of an individual's activities in the social environment, social and moral development constitute interrelated processes in which the moral evaluation needs arise.

The social environment and the family also play a role in the moral education of the child. Society, as a human creation based on the principles of morality and justice, seeks to direct the behavior of the child within certain forms and, in the case of a child, develop habits accordingly. On the other hand, a family with its own tradition, culture, and habits also shapes the behavior of the child.

Different psychological factors, as well as the factors of society and culture in which, in addition, the influence of the media, and the Internet as a medium, are intertwined in interaction with each other, so their influence on the moral development and moral behavior of the child can hardly be separated.

Future of Student's Ethics with AI and Computerized Learning

Moral education formulates principles and rules, which represent the most general requirements for moral behavior. The norms arising from the rules based on principles represent the concretization of moral principles. The best way to accept moral norms is precisely the concrete activity.

Thinking constitutes the essence of morality. Stages of reasoning are hierarchical structural units with an unchanging order of reporting. A goal of moral education is to set in motion the natural course of the moral development of the child. Moral development is a progression through the invariable sequence of development sequences, while moral maturity is the ability to independently reason and formulate moral principles.

The educational role of the elementary school is emphasized because education in elementary schools refers to the personality as a whole. At other levels of education, greater emphasis is placed on performing professional, and educational roles. Social interaction between teachers, students and teaching staff is the basis of education and education, and the general educational climate of the school is based on the quality of interpersonal relationships.

The preconditions of moral development include the creation of habits, conceptual understanding and language development, the ability to establish emotional relationships with others, the ability to participate in the activities that have rules, the relationships of teachers and students, and the social structure of the school.

The presumption for the transition to a higher stage of moral reasoning depends on two factors: 1. Challenges of moral conflict and disagreement over problematic situations; and 2. Expositions of the educators to the next stage of thinking, which is higher than the one at which the individual is present in this understanding, the role of teachers is to help the student to deal with moral problems, to think about the way to resolve moral conflicts, to see inconsistencies in their way of thinking. In this way, the student becomes aware of the adequacy of reasoning from a higher stage and in this way can overcome the inadequacy and inconsistency of their own thinking.

The value-neutral program of moral education is achieved by encouraging higher forms of moral reasoning, rather than by transferring content in the form of ideals, beliefs or codes of virtues.

Educational-moral goals and social-moral values are of particular importance in understanding moral education. The goals of moral education arise from those values that are significant to a particular society. There's an agreement on the value to be applied in the educational process is a question with no consensus in different countries. Although values such as legal tolerance, equality, enlightenment, and freedom appear most often, the way in which these values are manifested and manifested differs among different groups of people.

Moral upbringing is best accomplished with carefully selected contents, based on which moral principles, goals, and tasks are achieved. The most important areas of moral education include upbringing of general values, respect for work, ideological and political education, and patriotic education.

Values are classified in different ways, among others, terminal and instrumental. Variability is an important feature of value since they depend on the middle and position of the individual in that environment. Ideals, which penetrate all the doctrines of a particular society, penetrate both the values that depend on the social environment as well as the position of the individual within that environment. The common values, which will have the purpose of respecting differences, as well as promoting a common one, are necessary in addition to guiding to diversity.

The most common method of persuading, practicing, harassing and punishing is a critical norm. One should account for factors arising from the educator themselves and their individual features, the generally accepted goal and tasks of teaching, as well as the factors that derive from the teaching organization itself, such as the didactic-methodical goal of time, the time capacity for teaching and learning. There's also a dimension of the personality of the educators who make up the psychological basis of moral education, such as attitudes and beliefs of students, their readiness for cooperation, dignity, and honor, as well as the presence of general honesty of students.

Moral education programs should include content that will satisfy the different needs of the educator and his problems. They should include content that touches on the social orientation of the educators and the motives that the educators guide in their behavior.

Changes in the policy of computerized courses

It is necessary to design modern curricula in the direction of solving the problem, asking the question of how to reach a solution, and show independence in finding solutions. Democratic participation in education will expand the ability of critical thinking and active participation in gifted students, acquiring a comprehensive educational experience that includes the values and skills of educational, emotional and cognitive nature, which turns into collective learning. Media also plays an important role, which involves the evaluation, analysis, and knowledge of media activities and projects, exploring the systems of the influence of messages that are transmitted through the media to culture. The emphasis is on communication and collective work, which contributes to moral development. The use of information technology for the purpose of networking knowledge is what should shape modern school policies. In the context of connectionism theory, networking of information appears as a form of morally correct behavior, while retaining information for oneself is seen as a form of immoral behavior.

Basing the concept of computerized learning on the theory of connectionism, the emphasis is on fostering ethics, mutual respect, understanding and tolerance of diversity, accountability to others, which are characteristics that are very important for ethical behavior in virtual communities. Critical thinking is important in order to assess the accuracy and value of a lot of information available on the Internet, which can be accurate and scientific, but also incorrect, misleading and potentially dangerous.

Methods for detecting and sanctioning academic fraud and plagiarism

As a reaction to the worsening of the problem of plagiarism, copyright infringement and the general decline in ethics of behavior in academic and creative work, numerous techniques of detecting plagiarism have been developed over the last decades. This development has also contributed to the rapid development of information technology, as well as the growing awareness of ethical issues in science and education. The problem of plagiarism and academic fraud is seriously understood by scientists and officials of educational systems around the world, and they face it with the use of technology to detect plagiarism and cheating in academic work, but also by passing legislation, by sanctioning the education of students and teaching staff.

While the first forms of plagiarism detection were reduced to learning content compilation, recent methods of plagiarism detection include the use of software that identifies similarities in text phrases. Some of these tools are available for free use on the Internet (Small SEO tools, Viper, Plagiarism, Copy scape, etc.), and commercial programs that have content databases for detection of plagiarism (such as Turnitin.com) are also available. These programs can compare the content of a different volume with content published on the Internet as a whole, or with the content contained in the software databases.

As possible indicators of plagiarism, which can be perceived visually, I outline non-consistent citation styles, lack of quotes and allegations in long passages, unusual formatting, use of outdated language, use of complex vocabulary or terminology and irregularities in diction and style. In fact, students who were sanctioned by a grade reduction did not re-engage in further plagiarism, while the same number of students who were merely warned about it repeated the same violation. Caution is necessary for interpreting the results of automated software, taking into account that their testing has noted the possibility of obtaining false negative or false positive results, so they should be used only as indicators for further inspection of students' work.

Education of students

Learning based on problem solving, research, establishing relationships and relationships within the group and within the content, that is, the formation of learning as a process of two-way communication in the formation of new knowledge leads to a process of acquiring knowledge that is focused on seeking answers and self-evaluation, and accepting responsibility for the importance and learning outcomes.

Teachers must go further than educating students about plagiarism. Academic integrity is, first of all, a reflection of the moral values of both the teacher and the student, and their care is a reflection of the moral development of the student. Students should be instructed to foster awareness of the respect for the rights of others, in addition to educating them about valid rules, that is, prohibitions of copyright infringement.

In order to emphasize the connection of giftedness and creativity, which leads to investing a lot of effort into creative work and, consequently, a lesser appearance of plagiarism among gifted, it's important to note divergent thinking, which includes elaboration, originality, flexibility and fluency, and emphasize that these factors, or only divergent thinking, are what drives the behavior of gifted students. This ability allows the possibility of simultaneous understanding of the possibilities that lead to this original solution to the problem. Elaborateness, as a characteristic that needs to be emphasized in computerized education, leads to the internal connection of morality, characterized by the sense of unconditional, feeling for good, moral feeling, moment, autonomy, and conscience as sanctions.

Students, in addition to education on academic integrity, intellectual rights and the use of tools for detecting plagiarism in their daily work, need help, education, adequate use of sources, equally printed and computerized. Here I advocate workshops and discussions on these topics, as well as exercises that will help students identify examples of plagiarism in their own and others' work.

In this chapter, I tried to point out the emergence of dealing with plagiarism and academic fraud in computerized education, as well as the potential to use computerized courses to support positive moral growth in students. I was interested in discovering and giving a brief overview of the views in this area that touches on issues of appearance and type, the causes and effects that this type of non-ethical behavior can have on learning, but also the development of personality in general.

Impatience and easy discontinuation in finding adequate learning materials, disturbed concentration, or focusing, chronic superficiality and the formation of physical and mental laziness are the leading, alarming negative effects of superficial learning in an computerized environment, the negative impact of the speed of data transfer in learning by using computerized sources, and intolerance to waiting for answers or feedback as some of the negative effects. Performing multiple tasks at the same time (multitasking) damages the concentration of attention and negatively influences the depth of the processing of information related to the learning material. Learning by multitasking, in addition to requiring more time, is less efficient, leading to learning modes that are making it more and more difficult for students to concentrate on the particular idea they are studying and their ability to look deeper.

Frustration among students results in seeking an easier and faster path. Students encounter obstacles or fail in order to reach their goals in the shortest possible time. Students with these qualities easily give up research and turn around with well-trained, but superficial strategies.

It shouldn't be hard to understand the possible effect of negative factors on the rise in violations of moral and legal norms of copyright. The need to instantly find the necessary information, with their non-critical thinking, and not tolerating frustration among students, certainly influences their decisions to use unlawfully other's intellectual property.

In examining the causes and consequences of the non-ethical behavior of students in computerized education, I find it difficult to draw a clear line between the behaviors that occur as a cause, and those behaviors that emerge as a result of negative moral traits that leave participation in an accelerated, virtual world on some students. It seems that tolerance, patience, justice, and honesty, are virtues that can be built but can also suffer the negative impact of computerized media. Unfortunately, the findings of the study are in favor of the negative end of the spectrum, and what makes forms of behavior that lead to unethical behavior in computerized learning the cause and effect of this phenomenon is the fact that once they become successful, these behaviors are adopted as acceptable and repeated. The moral philosophy of students, it seems, becomes similar utilitarian and turned to one's self. In different ways, gaining a line of "lesser resistance" becomes a form of behavior, rather than an isolated case.

These phenomena have further negative implications on the significance and credibility of the acquired classifications as well as professional skills. Unfortunately, international and intercontinental communication also brings a collision between the laws of many countries, making the legal fight against copyright infringement almost impossible. To be precise, the market for copyright work most often implies the trade in intellectual work with a contractual obligation to transfer copyrights. The phenomenon of trade in student and scientific-research work skillfully escapes the plagiarism framework, but it still falls into a form of academic scam. In addition, this form of fraud is perfidious and potentially dangerous. In short, with a brief, but the internationally valid contract of part-time work, where (often in the ultimate financial necessity) the original author waives copyright in favor of the buyer, and a person who has not even participated in the creation of copyright work becomes its owner. This person can be a student, but also a scientist or doctor of science. There is no restriction on science fields that are subject to such trade, a type of fraud. With this knowledge, not only qualifications get acquired digitally, but also the quality of learning and education are questioned in general.

One of the best ways to change the attitudes, beliefs, habits, and behaviors of students is exactly moral education, that which covers all subjects and highlights communication at the level of one school. As the goal of moral education is the building of moral personality, it must be realized with constant work and content based on situations and dilemmas of real life. Accordingly, numerous authors have developed moral education programs that deal with different topics and apply different methods. The method of discussion and problem solving (dilemma) is distinguished as the most effective, provided that in a certain environment there is a permanent, well-designed, system of moral education based on democracy. In the context of intellectual work, training courses are important to teach students adequate writing and source research. Although these programs have proved to be effective to a certain extent, they have not yet significantly contributed to the reduction of plagiarism in experimental groups.

This can lead to one conclusion. In studying the problem of intellectual property rights violations by students, I encountered four important but isolated aspects. The first and the widest view involved the fight against plagiarism and academic fraud through the systematic, moral education of a whole personality. However, ideals, values, and related habits and behaviors cannot come to life in the student's mind only through the transmission of moral content. As a form of practical realization of the theory of moral education, there are also programs of moral education. These programs, in fact, had an effect to some extent. However, the difference is far from revolutionary. Another form of moral education is the education of students for proper writing of scientific contents, which also gives significant, but modest results. In the end, as a slightly more effective form of fighting against these forms of undesirable behavior, legal regulations emerge. As a reasonable conclusion, the idea is that none of these "strategies" in the fight against academic fraud and intellectual theft can give a significant result isolated and the absence of others.

In addition to the fact that students must internalize the values of justice, respect, honesty, and respect for others' property in all areas of life, they must receive such education in the school environment, in an organized form, backed up by the legal regulations that become more rigorous from year to year repel students in such behaviors. However, we cannot expect students to perform skills that they often do not have. In addition to moral education and ideology, the content of moral education at school and strict punishment of violations of standards, I must first provide students with the opportunity to build skills that are necessary for successful authoring work through education.

In this sense, I also need a space for studying several issues in this field. First of all, I consider that there is room and needs for studying the connection between plagiarism and education of students for research and writing, as well as the efficiency of applying strategies of positive motivation to negative ones. Namely, in addition to the fear of sanctions as possible "brakes" of the appearance of unwanted behavior, I see the space for using positive motivation, in the form of symbolic awards and merit for honest and diligent work of authorship. A sense of achievement and pride, monitored by the fact that they have created a properly written content worthy of academic status, certainly acts as a good impetus for just behavior.

AI learning and Informal education

Informal education, as a broad term, is a result of the practical application of different educational and learning theories and is sparked by technological progress and the development of educational technologies.

Essentially, informal education requires that a person independently organize his / her own learning. In this form of self-study, the student determines the beginning and the end of the work and values his own results. The rapid development of the information society has brought about major changes in the development and use of technologies used in the educational process. The affirmation of informal forms of education was the basis of the development of the concept of digital learning as a form of distance education that was independently guided. Prior to the emergence of digital learning, concepts of computer-based learning, Computer-based Assessments based on computer-based programs, software instruction, computer-assisted mentoring were instructed, etc., while machine learning is one of the newest concepts.

There's an emphasis on the importance of understanding versus memorization as the formulation of learning goals. Understanding occurs when information is organized around a key concept and can be applied in a multitude of other concepts. Learning is seen as an upgrade of previous knowledge that can be achieved through different approaches to learning in formal education. These approaches include lectures, group learning, project case studies, problems, projects, technologically advanced approaches, and learning based on skills development and training, contextual exercises and modeling. Since none of the learning modes can be considered the best, as each is applied in time and for the purpose for which it is most appropriate, the common goal of different forms of learning is to build and understand the whole of knowledge.

Among many existing types of learning, several particularly relate to the concept of informal education. Among these types, there's a distinction between active learning, situational learning, experiential learning, and relational learning. Since different learning theories are not strictly related to learning types, the general framework of the concept of non-formal education is composed of numerous forms of learning intertwined in its various categories. One example of this is integrative learning, which combines experimental and relational learning.

Unbiased assessment and evaluation (tests and exams)

Educational factors, in the eyes of many, include elements derived from teachers themselves from one instruction and on the other, as well as content factors. The factors that arise from the properties that the teacher carries within me include elements such as interaction with students, feedback, academic qualifications and professional development.

Virtual reality & personalized learning environment

The instructional design factors refer to elements such as cooperation and teamwork, engaging higher levels of cognitive structure of students, quality and diversity of learning resources, learning materials, active learning, learning activities, student motivation, design standards, evaluation, use of graphics and media, attractiveness of students, data rate and inclusiveness.

Content factors include an element such as the accuracy and relevance of the content, the content of the content, the renewal and improvement of the content.

Technological factors, by many, include elements such as a technological plan, quantity of available content, course infrastructure, technical support for students and lecturers, training for students and lecturers, adequate management of student data collection.

Students' factors that connect with the success of machine learning, such as communication with other students, time management, learning place, individual learning pace, efficiency and effectiveness expectations, thinking strategies, motivation, dedication, self-confidence, problem-solving skills.

Starting from the fact that computerized learning in its nature is enriched by various technological, educational, sociological, political and other factors, I have also looked at the way in which all these elements are united in the key factors of e-education. The computerized platform, that is, the interface, the teachers or the teaching staff and the students as the center of the entire process, are key factors in the machine learning process.

Taking this connection into account, encountering and mutually interweaving of different factors is inevitable. I tried to link different educational, technological and factors that emerge from the students' personality to be able to examine their interdependence. For this reason, analyzing the connections and the conditioning of factors that affect the effectiveness of eLearning will be the next task of my review.

Reflecting upon the systematization of the factors that affect the success in machine learning I have outlined in the previous chapter, it is evident that there are contact points between different human, educational and technological elements that make up a complex web.

Technology-driven instruction

The instructional design

Technological progress achieved in the field of education has influenced the increasing interaction between students and teachers, various technological tools and increasing interaction with digital content, as well as its role and connection with personal development. Understanding the role of PLEs in fostering motivation for learning, satisfaction and professional development, as they enable the use of different technologies and strategies for lifelong learning.

The term 'Web 2.0' is a new concept of Internet usage and its relationship with the education framework. This tool allows the creation of incentive environments, PLE. This concept is related to Learning Management Systems (LMS), and also to social networks (Academia.eu, ResearchGate, Twitter, Linkedin, Perltrees), as well as the concept of lifelong learning. PLE implements the key principles of eLearning 2.0, the autonomy and power of students, lifelong learning, sharing and collaboration, the value and importance of informal learning, the potential of social software, the understanding of networking as a space for socialization, knowledge, and learning.

Given the fact that the term is moderately new, there is still no commonly accepted definition of PLE. However, in exploring this notion, two important aspects from which he should be considered are highlighted. On the one hand, PLE is an approach based on the use of computerized tools, which I cannot consider as software, but an environment in which individuals, communities and resources communicate with each other in a flexible way through applications available on Web 2.0, whether it is an interactive software or not.

The second viewpoint relates to the fact that PLE can be introduced using technology, including applications and services, combined with interpersonal relationships within the network of contacts that are a key part of these environments.

Teachers, as participants, have structured content to provide an understanding of the content organization. The effective design of course content and resources is described as one of the important determinants of key content components and the course itself by trainees and teachers of post-secondary computerized courses.

It is considered that a properly thought-out system strengthens the participants' commitment to clear communication in the instructions and relevance of the content goals. Teachers also adapt their approach to individual and different learning styles of learners by providing multiple content interactions through discussion boards, joint activities, and resource-related resources, thus providing students with opportunities to approach content studies in a more personalized fashion.

Technological advancement

Technological factors, by many, include elements such as a technological plan, quantity of available content, course infrastructure, technical support for students and lecturers, training for students and lecturers, adequate management of student data collection.

Instructional design and technical support. The computerized environment is designed in such a way to provide the possibility of a fast and uninterrupted flow of information, data and digital educational material. Within the computerized environment, students have the opportunity to take educational materials in a few seconds or submit their own work on assessment. Therefore, course attendees have the opportunity to receive and send relevant data much faster and more practical than in the traditional sense. They do not have to leave their homes for the purpose of purchasing books or printing works, for example.

Only computer and internet access are required to participate in e-education programs. Given the more affordable prices of the program, students with lower incomes can afford it, and given that e-education does not require a change of place of residence and additional costs, it provides equal opportunities for students from different cultural and social backgrounds to study under equal conditions. Under such conditions, students have a chance to communicate with members from different countries, cultures and different social status. The mutual exchange of opinions and experiences among students helps them to enrich their cultural knowledge. In this way, students who come from economically and socially marginalized environments can expand their knowledge in ways in which they can't within their local environment. On the other hand, students who come from environments with high living standards can learn a lot about the real problems that their peers from other parts of the world encounter.

The computerized environment provides the possibility of distant communication, which means that students from different geographic locations are given the opportunity to participate in educational programs under equal conditions. Most of the computerized environments provide equal access and interaction between participants regardless of their geographic location. This provides participants around the world the opportunity to communicate with each other, using private messages, forums, and discussions. The possibility of global, international communication, helps students to observe the topics they are studying from different cultural perspectives, which can be very useful in the study of social sciences. Learning about the different cultural contexts of concepts, phenomena, philosophical settings and beliefs through discussion with other students within the computerized environment helps to widen the perspective and form a view of the fresh from different perspectives.

Instructive environments can have a positive impact on student motivation. These influences arise from the fast and concise nature of computerized communications, which enables timely information and feedback. The demands placed on students are clearly and precisely defined, so there is no danger of misinterpretation of instructions. Starting from the course guidance and material studies, tests and instructions for their completion, including a transparent assessment system, students are clearly informed of what is expected of them and what they have to do to achieve a satisfactory result.

For many e-learners, mastering system technology can be a challenge. Although most students are used to using computers, computerized systems require an understanding of the pace and schedule of activities, the resources needed, and how to deliver and access their own work. With those students who aren't equipped in this area, motivation may fall due to uncertainty about the correctness of one's own skills and methods. Interpreting feedback in these circumstances is difficult, and it can be especially stressful for a student who is not sure if something works properly or not. I can understand how difficult it is for a student who is not sure about the accuracy of his own work to concentrate fully on learning. Positive feedback and a sense of initial success are essential steps at the beginning of each education, at all ages. When this is denied to a student, we can expect negative effects on their motivation for learning.

The Internet is the medium on which the functioning of the entire computerized communication depends and the possibility of global connectivity. Although the Internet opens up many opportunities for connecting people from different geographic areas, its malfunction immediately prevents and interrupts every form of computerized communication, also denying access to sites and computerized education programs. The disadvantages in the proper functioning of the Internet can prevent students from regularly participating in all the activities of the computerized program, or take the exam. On the other hand, the malfunction of the Internet server by the administrator of the program can lead to paralysis of the whole system, the inability to publish content, ratings and many other problems.

Although most computerized education programs require students to access a computer, a much larger amount of technology is used on the side of the program administrator to function and maintain the system. Access to the computer is not equal to all students around the globe, although I are inclined to think that this is. A computer malfunction or some disadvantage in its functions can impair the student in regular work, as well as the failures of the devices on the administrator's side. There are many factors that can interfere with student communication with the organization in this regard, such as computer malfunction, slow downloading of downloadable files, inability to read part of messages or complete loss of access to the site.

Adjustability & Flexibility (instant updates and improvements)

The factors that emerge from the students themselves and teachers interact with one another in a way that ultimately determines the effectiveness of communication between teachers and pupils, and therefore the right interpretation of information and content by students. On the one hand, the educational approach and teacher qualifications directly influence the way in which they will form their own teaching work and instruction. From the technical training and readiness of the teachers, this method of communication with the student depends directly on the quality and the constructiveness of the feedback he provides.

On the other hand, student factors define the accuracy and success of interpreting feedback. Feedback, from the viewpoint of students, is in direct connection with motivation, as a decisive factor in learning success. Other factors that arise are students 'characteristics, especially time, place and individual learning rhythm, affect students' openness to teamwork and collaborative learning.

The instructional design factors work directly to shape the perception of students in relation to the course itself and its content. Since student satisfaction is an important factor of motivation for learning, conditioned by the observable usability, the usefulness of the course, the design of the instructional interface is one of the important factors that influence the interpretation of student feedback and motivation for learning.

The instructional design of computerized teaching cannot be viewed separately from the technological plan of the very platform of computerized education, therefore, its technological foundation.

Talent, Equality & Diversity

Technology forms the basis of computerized education and is the basis on which other educational elements are being upgraded. Technical support, the adequate preparation of both teachers and students for the tasks that they expect in this process, are key elements that influence the successful outcome of the entire process. Adequate student readiness to learn and work in computerized environments directly reflects on their motivation for learning, the correct understanding and interpretation of feedback, as well as the flow and success of interaction and communication in this process.

In analyzing the problem of this section, I encountered the challenges posed by the disciplinary dilemmas of scientific material related to computerized education. This notion is present in the study of various sciences, and the understanding of key concepts which varies with the discipline to which the content of education relates, and the educational aspects interweave with the findings of psychology, technology, and IT. Given the fact that computerized education is a kind of hybrid which, in a complex way, requires the merging and cooperation of experts from different fields of science, I estimate that for future work in this area a multidisciplinary approach to problems and aspects of computerized learning is needed. I find the need for a more detailed study of the aspects of social learning and self-regulation in the learning of computerized education, equally in a general form, as well as the study of the specific factors and elements that make it. In the scientific work of the experts, I notice significant progress in the study of these elements, however, a formal overview of these problems could lead to a significant improvement in the quality of the learning process in computerized courses. Furthermore, the field of social learning in computerized teaching as well as the possibility of computerized teaching in the formation of knowledge, skills, and habits that go beyond the informative content of the course also deserves greater scientific attention, for the reason that I will state as the ultimate conclusion of our discussion. Namely, you mustn't forget that teaching, besides the material, has its own functional and educational tasks, and the "knowledge" acquired by respecting only its material aspect is not and cannot be considered a true knowledge.

Virtual Reality and Augmented Reality in Education

The area of computerized education is rapidly developing at the present time. The development of e-universities, individual educational courses, as well as the opening of universities around the world to the possibilities of computerized education through the design of computerized courses, is conditioned but also accompanied by numerous scientific studies.

E-Learning Communication for Students: Is Digital as Effective as Direct?

Computerized education is a blend of the achievements of various sciences, and from the educational angle, we have decided to look into the advantages and weaknesses of interaction and communication in the computerized environment from the viewpoint of the students.

This subject arises from the understanding of the importance of communication for the success of the learning process and the achievement of favorable educational results. This subject also arises from the fact that the nature of communication by computerized means is different from other forms of communication, which is meaningful in the educational context. In the following, we will search for the answer to the question: "What are the advantages and disadvantages of communicating a student (learner) in a computerized environment?"

E-Learning Communication: The Real Effects of Virtual Reality

We studied the problem of the advantages and weaknesses of communication in the computerized environment through the study of scientific sections and published texts of experts from different fields of science. In these studies, findings from the field of information technology and designing educational courses prevail, and the challenge to interpret the reflections in the field of information technologies in the educational context.

What is Virtual Reality?

A virtual environment can be defined as a computerized space in which a person engages in real-life experiences.

For users of virtual environments, experiences are made possible through simulations, situations, and events from another location, while they are physically present in another. When multiple individuals participate in the same activity within a single virtual space, they often form virtual cultural groups. The most obvious example for this would be gaming communities, in which avid game players form relationships that begin as dependent on the role in the game, but often grow into real-life distant friendships. In terms of e-learning, groups of students share the same learning interface, forming a diverse virtual group/team.

In many ways, the communities of students and teachers in computerized education programs are virtual communities. Within the frames of a common panel, members of this community spend a certain number of hours during the day and week of work, performing tasks, in which the designed user interface replaces the university building.

Educational Framework of Virtual reality

In order to achieve its philosophy application and quality of learning in computerized education, the development of educational technology, enhanced by the potentialities of ICT, is an important but not sufficient guarantee for it.

Due to the increase in the number of students, lecturers are exposed to an increase in the number of students, which can impair the quality of teaching. In these conditions, the time available for training to work on new learning technologies is getting smaller, and the quality of the process of teaching and evaluating student work is decreasing.

The educational framework is composed of four hierarchically connected elements: philosophy, high-level pedagogy, strategies, and educational tactics.

Philosophy of Education

At the top of the hierarchical pyramid, there is a philosophy, which consists of beliefs about the aspects essential for education. Answering important questions, such as:

Understanding the nature of knowledge and competencies,

Understanding the process of learning process and attitudes toward students,

Educational philosophy determines the concept of education that will shape the entire course.

Disagreements within the expert team on the key philosophical aspects of the education process lead to harmful divergences in the daily cooperation between teachers and students. In everyday communication between teachers and students it is important to understand the meanings of terms from the perspective of the other, so the discord in the work team on this issue may result in mixed messages being sent to students.

High-level learning

High-level learning provides an understanding of the key concepts of machine learning, so it relates to the views of learning that form their own branches, such as:

Learning through discovery,

Problem-based learning or computer-related collaborative learning.

High-level concepts are found between abstract ideas and the practical use of knowledge, steering the e-course in a certain direction in terms of values and educational philosophy.

E-Course Strategy

The strategy is closest to practice and refers to a detailed description of a plan or strategy for performing certain tasks. The strategy enables the identification and clarification of those points that can cause confusion in the work team and lead to misunderstanding and disagreement in communication between teachers and students.

Learning motivation in virtual reality

The very nature of computerized education can have positive and negative effects on the motivation of learners. These influences can arise from the nature of interaction specific to this form of education and the way students communicate with the system (interface), teachers and other students

Some of the negative effects on the motivation for learning are related to the lack of direct communication between students and teachers that can lead to feelings of frustration, isolation, and insecurity in the quality and correctness of their work.

For many e-learners, mastering system technology can be a challenge. Although most students are used to computers, computerized systems require an understanding of the flow and schedule of activities, the resources needed, how to deliver and enter their own work. In those students who are unequipped in this area, motivation may reduce due to uncertainty about the correctness of one's own work and procedures.

Obtaining feedback in these circumstances is difficult, and can be particularly stressful for a student who is not sure whether he is doing something right or not. We can understand how difficult it is for a student who is not sure about the correctness of his own work to concentrate fully on work. Positive feedback and a sense of initial success are essential steps towards learning at all ages. When this is denied to a student, we can expect negative effects on their motivation.

Man, as a social being, naturally seeks to establish contacts and associate with other people for the purpose of working together and achieving a goal. Learning is a social process, so most students prefer to exchange impressions, information, and explanations with their peers. When the student is isolated from the group, and if the educational program does not offer the possibility of group work and mutual counseling, interest and motivation for learning can degrade.

Competitiveness and Teacher Authority

The competitive spirit and the need for students to compare each other in order to understand their own place in relation to others are very noticeable in traditional higher education. Most computerized education programs do not provide this possibility, which can affect students' motivation and their need for achievement.

The authority of the experts under, that is, trust and respect for that person (be it a teacher or an author) plays a big role in the amount of effort that students will invest in learning. Due to the lack of direct contact between teachers and students, trust in the authors of the content of the program is under question.

On the other hand, learning via the Internet can have positive effects on student motivation. Positive influences stem from the precise nature of digital communication, which enables timely information and feedback.

How E-Learning Keeps Students Motivated

First, the demands placed on the students are clearly and precisely defined, so there is no danger of misinterpreting the instructions advertised online. Beginning of the course guidance and material studies, tests and instructions for their completion, including a transparent assessment system, students are clearly informed of what is expected of them and what they have to do to achieve a satisfactory result.

What does the research say?

Computerized education systems, in most cases, leave a positive impression on students. Students then form positive attitudes and expectations towards e-education in general, which improves their motivation to join in some future forms of computerized education.

Future of AI: Challenges of communication in a computerized environment

There are many factors that can interfere with student communication with the organization in this regard, such as computer malfunction, slow downloading of downloadable files, inability to read parts of messages or complete loss of access to the site.

Starting from the philosophical commitment of the course's author, which provides a framework for understanding the interrelations of teachers and students, through a high-level pedagogy that determines the understanding of key concepts of education and education, to educational strategies and tactics that most directly relate to the organization and implementation of educational tasks in the process of computerized education, we outlined certain requirements regarding the regulation of communication in the computerized environment.

Freedom from authority

Discussions, forums, e-mails, and other forms of digital communication all have one thing in common: a sense of mental distance from the person on the opposite side of the screen. When it comes to e-students, this psychological distance has both a positive and a negative effect:

POSITIVE: Students feel less nervous when communication isn't direct, and they have enough time to prepare;
NEGATIVE: In this type of 'class climate', students may lack the ability to phrase their questions and answers clearly enough for their teachers and peers to understand;

Still, it is noted at advantages exceed the shortcomings in terms of less fear of authority. Student's feel more freedom of personal expression in a semi-formal environment. As a result, their work is organized better and they appear to phrase questions clearly and concisely.

Remote communication

Digital learning environment provides all the students in the group to access the course at their convenience (be it from home, library computer, or any other computer), all under receiving equal, uniformed conditions as other members of the group.

Most of the computerized environments provide equal access and interaction between participants regardless of their geographic location. This provides participants around the world the opportunity to communicate with each other, using private messages, forums, and discussions. This possibility of global, international communication helps students analyze the problems they are studying from different cultural perspectives, which has beneficial effects on their intercultural communication skills. Arguably, being able to look at subject topics through the lens of different cultural contexts helps students prepare for a future, diverse work environment.

Learning about the different cultural contexts, phenomena, philosophical settings and beliefs through discussion with other students within the digital environment helps to widen the perspective and form a view of the fresh from different perspectives.

Fast and easy data transfer

The computerized learning environment is designed in such a way to provide the possibility for a fast and uninterrupted flow of information, data and digital educational material. Within the computerized environment, students have the opportunity to download educational materials in a few seconds and to submit their own work for assessment. Therefore, course attendees have the opportunity to receive and send relevant data much faster and easier than in the traditional sense. They do not have to leave their homes for the purpose of purchasing books or printing papers.

Lack of non-verbal communication elements

Facial expression, mimics, body language, and tone are important in understanding the connotative meaning of exchanged messages. If these elements are missing, communication is deprived of emotional and affective elements. Also, when communication is deprived of non-verbal elements, errors in the interpretation of messages are possible, which can lead to confusion in the conversation. The very lack of emotional and affective elements of communication can negatively affect the motivation for learning.

In digital communication, which, while providing opportunities for more organized and more efficient messaging, is still lacking in the spontaneity of the natural conversation. Providing illustrations and examples related to the topic is made more difficult since a teacher can't observe student's reactions to make sure if they understood examples and metaphors.

Lack of face-to-face communication

Electronic communication also has a more formal tone than direct communication, so many elements of spontaneous communication are lost. This makes further clarification of misunderstandings that more difficult. These disadvantages in electronic education are first reflected in problems of understanding computerized messages and instructions given within the user interface. Misunderstanding or incomprehensible understanding of given instructions makes the work of course participants more difficult, adversely affecting their motivation for work and leading to poorer learning results.

Internet dependency

The Internet is the medium which depends on the functioning of all computerized communications and the possibility of global connectivity. Although the Internet opens up many opportunities for connecting people from different geographic areas, its lack or malfunction immediately prevents and interrupts every form of computerized communication, aside from limiting access to sites and e-learning programs. The lack of a stable internet connection can prevent students from regularly participating in all the activities of the computerized program, or taking an exam. On the other hand, the malfunction of the Internet server by the administrator of the program can lead to paralysis of the whole system, leading the inability to publish content, ratings and many other problems.

Dependence on technology

Although most computerized education programs require trainees to have computer access, the administrator of the program uses a more extensive amount of technology designed to maintain the system and keep it running. Access to the computer is not equally easy for all students around the world, although we like to think that it is. A computer malfunction or some disadvantage in its functions can undermine the student's regular work, as do the failures of the devices on the administrator's side.

Future Suggestions for Improving E-learning ICT Efficiency

We can conclude that text messages that the user interface and course administrators need to be clear, concise and well organized to allow for a clearer understanding by the student.

Messages received by students relate to the goals and tasks of work, explanations, instructions, and notices, and we have therefore concluded that the educational framework of computerized communications in a virtual environment determines the efficiency of understanding messages and the information that is transmitted. Thus, direct and indirect messages received by students are conditioned by the educational conception of a particular computerized course.

- The communication and interaction of students within computerized research involve students' communications with the system, the community of other students and the professor.

- This communication usually takes place through discussions, forums, e-mails or personal messages, and the system itself communicates passively with the student through notifications and instructions published on the course site.

- This network of communication is certainly different from its traditional "earthly" vision, which is qualitatively completely different.

- Communication within the computerized environment occurs through the Internet and that it is conditioned by the course rules and secured resources within the user interface. This kind of communication takes place remotely, more precisely, between participants who do not reside in the same physical space and do not have direct contact face to face.

- Computerized communication takes place in writing and provides the possibility of transferring text and digital files among the participants.

Accessibility is amongst the most important advantages of computerized communications within a virtual environment, regardless of geographical location, and the possibility of involving students from different socio-cultural backgrounds. Digital communication definitely erases geographic borders, whether it's cities, states or continents. It provides equal access and opportunities to all registered students irrespective of the environment from which they originate, which leads us to the next item, which is the equal opportunity for students from different socio-cultural backgrounds.

We know that cultural environments, and especially social circumstances, affect students' educational abilities. In an environment that provides equal opportunities for everyone, students are enabled to communicate with the community and their professors unencumbered by the limitations their social circumstances imply. This is especially important for students from marginalized social environments, where there are neither sufficient resources nor sufficient incentives to learn, or education is not sufficiently evaluated.

Communication in digital environments also provides fast, accurate and clear feedback on student work. Unlike traditional education, a student is not required a specific waiting period or personal appearance at the institution to receive feedback. This way, the student uses his own time more effectively, and the feedback he receives is designed in advance to provide a better understanding. An additional advantage of computerized communications in this context is the ability to quickly and easily transfer data, whether they are textual or multimedia. In this regard, students are facilitated access to educational content and delivery of copies of their own work, since there is no requirement for copying material and visiting the school.

Although the advantages of communication within the computerized environment are numerous and significant, in practice, notable shortcomings of this form of communication are present. One of the disadvantages is the lack of direct communication, which has its negative consequences, despite the numerous benefits of international connectivity through distance learning. Namely, the absence of direct communication is accompanied by the deprivation of elements of nonverbal communication and emotional elements that make face-to-face communication effective. These elements give a certain context and allow participants to see and appreciate the individual characteristics and circumstances of the other. When these elements miss out, misunderstandings are possible that may result in misinterpretations of messages, instructions, and feedback from a student.

With all its benefits, computerized communication depends on the proper functioning of the Internet and the accompanying technology. Any malfunctions or malfunctions may result in harmful consequences for the functioning of the entire education program or prevent the student from contacting the program as an entire system, teacher or other students.

In considering the advantages and disadvantages of student communication within the computerized environment, we can conclude that the positive and negative effects of this kind of communication depend in particular on the individual characteristics of students. We believe that adaptability to the use of new technologies, verbal fluency that influences the ability to adequately communicate thoughts in writing, and the characteristics of the personality that determines communication are essential factors that will determine student's success in communication within the computerized environment. The same factors that affect the effectiveness of direct communication, in our opinion, affect the effectiveness of computerized communication.

The effectiveness of student communication and interaction within the computerized environment, in our opinion, depends on the level of education for the use of computers and the use of the Internet, which in many cases does not have to be conditioned by the aforementioned individual characteristics. It is known that many successful, eloquent and highly educated experts sometimes encounter obstacles to the use of digital assets, and the same goes for students. The skills of using the Internet and handling the computer are formed through organized educational work and within family education, and their lack or absence can make the student's work considerably more difficult.

In the end, through the analysis of this problem, we encountered certain issues, which we consider worthy of additional analysis. In the first place, in order to improve the quality of communication in the computerized environment, we consider that further study of the influence of individual personality characteristics of a student on the effectiveness of communication in computerized education will shed light on many issues of positive and negative effects of distance communication and help creators of computerized education programs to make their design and functions adapt in such a way to stimulate students of different characteristics to a successful communication. The adequate education of students for the use of electronic education systems and learning within the computerized environment is an essential determinant of the success not only of communication in this field but also of the process of computerized learning in general.

Online education theories and models

Constructive Learning as General Framework

The constructivist theory gives the general framework and a prospective influence in terms of the way the learning process itself is viewed. This approach recognizes the previous knowledge and understanding with which participants' access the learning situation.

Learning occurs through active learning and integration of newly acquired and past knowledge and experience. Many of these perceptions are the result of experiential learning. Within this framework, learning is supposed to spark positive social changes as it doesn't only stop at intellectual knowledge.

The abstract ideas are expected to cause permanent behavior changes and lead to action, resulting in the overall progress of mankind.

Constructivism introduces the idea that a student composes their own knowledge. It's not embedded into their mind like one store's data on a computer. Each student creates one's own individual and social ideas during the learning process. In essence, learning is the construction of meaning.

As a result, there is a need to direct students to reflect on the learning process itself (meta-learning), and to the fact that there is no learning and knowledge that is separate from the meaning that the student interprets in his individual and social experience. This also applies to student communities, such as class communities.

Accepting the constructivist theory of learning requires moving away from realistic views of epistemology and accepting the views on knowledge as both student's independent act, and the construct of the one who teaches.

Learning does not imply an understanding of the true nature of things and phenomena that are being studied, nor the recollection of ideas from the past, but merely the personal and social meaning of a series of sensations, stimuli, which do not possess a meaning except for the meaning given to them by the student.

Main Principles of Constructivist Theory of Learning

The guiding principles of constructivism, which relate to the role of teachers, are based on the belief that learning consists of constructed meanings within the individual. These principles can help organize non-formal learning programs, such as learning in a museum.

1. Learning is an active process

The first principle is that learning is an active process in which a student uses sensory receptors and constructs knowledge based on them. A more traditional formulation of this principle includes the term 'active learning', which emphasizes that a learner in the learning process must be active, that is, they have to engage in certain activities. Learning cannot be viewed as a mere acquisition of knowledge; It involves the active interaction and engagement of students with the world and the environment.

2. Learning is a construct of both meaning and the meaning systems

The second principle stems from the view that the learning process consists of equally constructing the meaning and constructing of a meaning system. In this way, the student learns to learn during the learning process. The earlier construction of meaning helps in constructing the meaning and understanding of the meaning of other sensations that correspond to a similar particular pattern.

3. The importance of subconscious learning

The third principle of constructive teaching refers to the view that the most important, key step in constructing the meaning of the subconscious. Direct activity and engagement, as well as direct experience, necessary for learning, especially in children, are not sufficient in themselves. For successful learning, it is necessary to engage the mind, next to the hand. This is called reflexive activity. In the context of learning, the reflexive activity involves internal invention, analysis, and conclusion based on received sanctions from the outside world. It implies the activity of the mind, in addition to the activity of the hand.

4. Language of Learning

The fourth principle refers to the language of learning. Language, in itself, influences the learning process, and the researchers have noticed that people speak to themselves in the course of learning, that is, they turn to themselves.

5. Learning is a Social Activity

The fifth principle relates to the fact that learning is a social activity, closely and inseparably linked to the relationship of the individual with the surrounding people. The groups in which a person belongs are peers, other students in the group, teachers, family, and friends, as well as acquaintances.

Recognizing and appreciating this fact brings greater success in learning than avoiding it. Sensitivity is opposed to traditional learning practice that isolates pupils from social interaction, observing the education process as a one-sided relationship of the individual with the content of learning.

The progressive concept of education recognizes the social aspect of learning, using discussions, conversation, and interaction with others, as well as the application of knowledge as an integral aspect of learning.

6. Context of Learning

The sixth principle of constructive learning relates to the contextuality (mix) of learning. Learning does not take place isolated from the world and life, but rather in relation to previous knowledge, beliefs, prejudices, and fears. This idea correlates with the view that learning is an active process, an integral part of human life. It is a social process that cannot be separated from social experience, the world, and life. It is impossible to separate learning from life, and especially from the personal lives of students.

7. Learning Requires Past Knowledge

The seventh principle implies that learning requires previous knowledge. It is impossible to build new knowledge without its foundation on previously acquired knowledge. Knowledge acquired is an upgrade of previously acquired knowledge, and greater previous knowledge enables better acquiring knowledge and learning in the present. Consequently, teachers' efforts must be directed toward individual states of students and directed towards his previously acquired knowledge.

8. Learning Takes Time

The eighth principle expresses the fact that learning requires time, it is not a momentary process. In order to build a system of meaning, that is, knowledge, the task of students is reflected in the repetitive analysis of experiences and reflection. Even moments of deep insight can be traced back to the long preparation periods that preceded them. In the context of informal learning, short-term exposure of a student to an object or an event is not sufficient to form a system of meanings, but it is necessary to have multiple exposures that allow a student to reflect and contemplate experience.

9. The Importance of Motivation

The ninth principle states that motivation in learning is a key component essential to learning, in addition to helping the learning process. Motivation in this concept is taken as a factor that involves understanding how knowledge can be used.

Modern age demands to students learn based on a deep understanding and mastering relevant knowledge, information, and skills. Knowledge must be relevant and easy to connect and apply.

The direction of the educational process focuses on learning to learn, develop the skills of independent thinking and forming positive attitudes towards lifelong learning. Unlike traditional education, which highlights success, the modern concept of education sees success in learning from the aspect of skills development.

Constructivism: Connections between School Knowledge and Real-Life Experiences

A traditional view on education has led to situations where students are not able to apply acquired knowledge, as well as to form meaningful relationships between different concepts, easily forgetting the acquired knowledge. Even students who achieve high results on standardized tests are often unable to establish a link between the knowledge gained in class and real-life situations and experiences.

The constructivist theory, in general, is a set of different theoretical approaches. The term itself, constructivism, is most often used for the purpose of reviewing the key assertions of scientific realism, namely that objects of knowledge exist independently of the mind that observes them, and the second is that scientific claims of truth about the outside world.

In accordance with the general idea of constructivism, which states that each person constructs an independent reality, and according to different reference positions, various forms of constructivism can be found in the literature.

Individual VS Social Constructivism

Since numerous constructivist trends in literature interpret constructivism in various ways while directing and emphasizing various aspects of learning and personality development, these theories can be roughly separated into two currents, and on the basis of whether they regard learning as an individual or social process. On the one hand, the continuum contains individual constructivist theories, which view learning as an individual process, which takes place within the individual and his unique experiences and constructs. On the other hand, social constructivism views learning as a social process within which individuals learn from one another and one among others while changing reality.

Although these two theories of constructivism contrast significantly, it is common for them to emphasize the active knowledge acquisition, whereby the knowledgeable subject actively participates in the construction of knowledge.

Digital Learning & Individual Student Characteristics

Digital learning differs from the learning environment outside the classroom, thus putting teachers or instructors into a position where they have to use special ways of observation and technique to help students achieve success. The needs of students of different ages vary, so the characteristics that teachers have to observe in order to respond to their individual characteristics are different. Changes also reflect the philosophy and methodology of learning in such a way that they require changes in the qualitative nature of the instruction itself.

Recognizing the individual characteristics of students is among the most important factors that influence the success and outcomes of computerized learning.

The Risks of 'Television Learning'

The danger of so-called television learning, where a student passively observes computerized content, is that it causes boredom, in addition to other negative effects, such as reduced learning depth and motivation for learning.

In addition to this, the active role of participants in education that motivates to actions in which digital content is understood, interpreted, applied and discussed. To successfully pass the passivation of learning, the role of teachers is shifted from the source of knowledge to the mentor in acquiring knowledge. Activating the participants is, therefore, more important considering the results of the research, according to which most adult learners of computerized education have to overcome many obstacles in their everyday life obligations, in order to find and set aside time for computerized learning in their schedules.

Active learning

The continuum from passive to active learning is one of the significant dimensions of formal education. Nowadays emphasis is on the importance of active learning, in which the student is in direct interaction with the content. Here, the teacher is a supervisor whose role is reflected in the regulation of the process by designing and facilitating learning experiences.

Active learning is seen as the best form of educational practice whose strategies include reflection, active engagement, problem-solving, constructive learning, and interaction.

Although active learning still involves lectures as a form of education necessary in relation to content, it still involves reflection, problem-solving, and practical application of knowledge.

Situational learning

Situational learning implies and emphasizes the complex connection between the environment and the learning itself. From the aspect of constructivism, situational learning views the building of knowledge that occurs in the interaction of the individual with their legacy from previous experiences and the current environment/circumstances. This concept deems the importance of the observation of students in a social context, even in terms of external participation in situations where direct participation is not possible.

This kind of participation in communities is applicable in many situations of both formal and non-formal education. The connection between situational and experiential learning is noticeable, and can also be viewed as learning within the social context of a specific community, as well as in any other environment.

Experiential learning

Experiential learning implies learning through actions, the simplest way, and the key moment of experiential learning is the one in which an individual learns through action instead of observation.

Many view experiential learning as an active process of dealing with the circumstances and problems of the world that surrounds an individual. In this process, the individual first creates and then tests different solutions through present experience and interaction with the environment in order to build awareness of their own progress. This helps teachers develop a model of experiential learning that takes place in four the phases: observation, reflection, formation, and abstract concepts and generalizations of concepts in new situations.

This model of experiential learning leads to increased engagement and critical thinking. The very act of reflection emphasizes as a fundamental, essential element of learning.

The role of reflection is to enhance the experience of informal learning and empower learning different types of content.

What makes the reflection pivotal in experimental learning is enabling the creation of meaningful ties with previous experiences leading to the development of innovative viewpoints, as a result of the transformative learning that leads to the knowledge internalization. Experiential learning can also occur in situations of informal learning. It can be designed and directed in the way it is done in formal education and outside school settings.

Relational learning

Relational learning occurs primarily in a social context where people use previously acquired social experiences in new situations by observing others. This principle is also called "observational learning" and is included in the theory of social learning. Observational learning involves the selection and adoption of behavioral roles by the learner.

Relational learning can include learning in small groups, learning by mentoring, learning from other participants in different communities. Communication is a key concept here. Relational learning can lead to reflexive thinking and improved retention of knowledge. It can have a transformative character, as a new perspective that changes the way students think, and it can also lead to improved learning abilities in new situations.

Future market changes

Demand for High-qualified expertise

As a way of gaining both formal and non-formal skills, machine learning has been a subject of research from many fields, including pedagogy, psychology, social science, and others. However, the place that machine learning assumes among different forms and levels of education is a topic discussed by many, with very little consensus.

It seems that machine learning, as a term, has a different meaning when observed as an individual form or a method of education. Where does machine learning belong on the map of key educational terms and definitions? To discuss this issue, one must first understand key guidelines that separate formal from non-formal and informal education, as well as the place machine learning, holds amongst them. The majority of authors discussing this topic focused on the matter of whether or not official institutions acknowledge the skills and qualifications gained with machine learning, and to what degree. Researchers also studied the possibilities of machine learning in providing knowledge, skills, and qualifications necessary to survive in the competitive business world.

While some place machine learning with institutionalized, formal education (include e-courses from universities), other place machine learning with non-formal and informal learning (recreational courses and seminars, as well as e-museums, galleries and libraries.

Non-Formal Education

Compared to formal education, non-formal education takes place outside the frames formal education but still complements it. Non-formal education aims to improve, upgrade, those skills and knowledge gained in formal education.

Similar to that, informal education is a form of education in which a student assumes a leading role in planning, scheduling and guiding their own learning process.

Machine learning, on the other hand, places computerized media as an intermediate between a teacher and a student, which is one of the qualities unique to this form of education.

This stands both for communication, as well as delivery of the learning content.

Formal VS Non-Formal Education

To analyze the role of machine learning in informal education, one must first understand the qualities and key elements that separate formal and informal education.

Non-Formal Education: Team Learning, Personal, and Professional Development

First, non-formal education is a process aimed to result in both personal and professional development. Elements such as responsibility for the learning outcomes and the very process, feedback and motivation, as well as democratic values, separate non-formal from informal learning.

Team learning is common in non-formal learning but is also becoming an increasingly valued form of learning in formal education as well. What brings formal and non-formal learning closer together is curriculum based on the needs of society, as well as participants.

Informal Learning: Student in the Center, Self-Guided

Many argue that non-formal education serves mainly to improve, upgrade, skills and qualifications gained in formal, institutionalized learning. Placing a student in the very center of the learning process is a unique quality to informal learning. While formal learning accents system norms and regulations, builds a curriculum around the system and positions a student into complying with these regulations, informal learning does exactly the opposite. It places a student in the center of the learning process, building a curriculum around student's educational and personal needs.

Students access informal education independently and have the option to abandon it without any repercussions. Student satisfaction plays a major role as well.

On the other hand, one may argue that formal education is no less based on willing participation and revolved around student satisfaction. More so than ever, modern institutionalized education is open to new possibilities, alternative methods of teaching and evaluating knowledge.

We can't deny that institutionalized systems have played a major role in researching, as well as applying modern knowledge. On all levels, institutionalized learning is based on willing participation and competitiveness among individuals' schools and universities.

Student-Teacher Interaction

Teacher-student relationship is different in formal and informal education. Institutionalized education places teacher and students into a hierarchy that subordinates a student, while non-formal education places a student and a teacher in an equal position. They are partners in the learning process, and the role of the teacher is to guide the student in building knowledge.

But, we can bring these to question as well. Modern institutionalized education also aims to improve communication and relationship between students and teachers, putting them into a more equal position. Modern education aims to bring teachers and students closer together in terms of communication as well as teaching.

Formal Education: Institutionalized Qualifications

Formal institutions acknowledge only qualifications gained with institutionalized education, in forms of certification and validation. Elements of technology and digital applications penetrating into formal education blur the lines between formal, non-formal and informal education.

Virtual Reality in Formal, Non-Formal, and Informal Education

Virtual, digital reality integrates with educational reality in forms of databases, machine learning, digital content, and many other forms. Arguably, we can say that, in modern days, every form of education had gained its computerized form. On the other hand, educational systems worldwide are depending on computerized databases for over a decade.

Digital museums are bringing formal and informal education closer together.

We tried to determine the place of computerized education in the function of informal education, and in order to find the answer to this question, we first explored the differences between formal and non-formal education.

The relation between formal and non-formal education, that is, the boundaries on which one ends and the other starts, is the framework for determining the place of computerized education in them, as well as within the informal education. Namely, the demarcation of the formal form of non-formal education, that is, the differentiation of one another, allows us to better understand the importance of various forms of computerized education, and in particular some of its aspects, such as recognition, representation, and knowledge in the formation of knowledge, skills, and qualifications.

In order to successfully examine computerized education in the function of informal education, we must review its place in formal and non-formal education.

Main Differences between Formal and Informal Education

Starting from establishing the lines between formal and informal education, we have identified the basic characteristics of non-formal education, namely voluntary participation, personal and professional development, group learning, , curriculum based on the needs of society and participants, and for the learning process very important trained and qualified educators.

Non-formal education is also a specific and flexible structure of plans and programs, a foundation on democratic values and shared responsibility for the learning outcomes between the leader and the group empowering participants.

In addition to focusing on empowering participants and building on democratic values, the qualities that bring formal and informal education together are that learning takes place within the group, as group work is also an integral part of teaching within formal education institutions. Establishing an educational program on the needs of the society and participants and the necessary qualifications of educators, are also characteristics that are common to informal and formal education.

Non-Formal Education: Upgrade of Skills

Considering the definition of non-formal education, according to which it serves the purpose of upgrading existing knowledge and skills, improving cognitive skills, upgrading knowledge and skills acquired by attaining formal education as well as acquiring those knowledge and skills that were not covered by formal education, we can establish that one of the characteristics which define these two forms of education is the fact that non-formal education most often serves as an upgrade of skills and knowledge acquired through formal education.

Significant differences in formal and non-formal education have also been found in the fact that non-formal education is more oriented towards the student than the formal one, taking into account the fact that individual forms of non-formal education can be accessed on their own initiative and can leave them alone without serious consequences.

Since the success and reputation of various forms of non-formal education is relevant and satisfaction, the assessment of the previous participants, a greater focus on the student is quite understandable.

Qualifications & Employability

For the prestige and reputation, and therefore the popularity of formal education institutions, the key criteria remain the quality of acquired qualifications and employability, while student/student satisfaction is not at the forefront, which explains the greater orientation of non-formal education to students from formal education.

The relationship between students and teachers, or course leaders, is different than in non-formal education. These differences are reflected in the fact that in institutional education they are hierarchically set up so that the teacher is superior to the position of the student.

In non-formal education, the courses are more adapted to the needs of students, and the interaction and communication between participants and program leaders are less formal than in institutional education.

We conclude that findings of similarities and differences in formal and non-formal education can be questioned, taking into account that modern changes in institutional education also entail the improvement of relations between teachers and students, and the primacy in the philosophy of education takes over those scientific theories that emphasize the relation of equality and trust between teachers and students.

One of our conclusions in studying the similarities and differences between formal and non-formal education is that the authorities in the field of employment mainly take into account only competences and skills acquired through formal education.

We can conclude that the formal recognition of professional competences and relevance is a crucial recognition of education by state authorities. It is guaranteed with formal education, while knowledge and skills acquired by non-formal education of the state are most often not recognized when it comes to professional titles. We believe that this is one of the most significant and crucial differences between formal and non-formal education.

The modern influences of technology and technological applications that penetrate the field of education and pedagogy make the boundaries of formal, non-formal and informal education foggy and often unclear. Modern educational reality has become closely connected to virtual reality.

Although nowadays, every form of education has acquired its computerized form and elements of machine learning, whether it is an informal self-improvement by reading computerized sources, attending computerized courses or obtaining a formal diploma by attending computerized universities, educational systems on the domestic terrain as well as other parts of the world, such as western Europe and America, largely depend on computerized databases to store and share scientific and educational materials, information and data.

Most authors place e-education within the framework of non-formal education, assuming that e-education includes forms of non-formal education such as seminars and computerized courses.

However, computerized education also includes many other forms of education, such as virtual museums and communities dedicated to informing about various scientific and non-academic topics, such as internet forums, computerized journals, websites and blogs of individuals and organizations affiliated in the interests of specific topics.

We conclude that the authors mainly recognize several forms of computerized education that can be introduced under the framework of non-formal education, while numerous and significant achievements in the development of this field, which come from the field of informal education, such as virtual museums, galleries, and computerized scientific journals, often make their analysis more difficult.

Digital education is, first of all, a learning process that utilizes computerized media, which is a factor that can make it an integral part of formal, non-formal or informal education. Computerized education can be part of formal education systems in the form of applications and panels within institutional education, it can be one of the specific forms of non-formal education in the form of computerized courses and seminars. Computerized education can also be one of the forms of informal education if the computerized media is used for the purpose of independent and self-initiative education through the study of cultural and scientific contents.

Future Skills in Education

Are current jobs safe from automation? Are we at the brink of a future in which human labor will be completely replaced by machines? If so, what are the modern demands in terms of e-learning, and how can we adopt the modern curriculum to secure the students with future employment?

While economist, psychologists, and experts on social studies focus on matters of workplace diversity and equality, the experts in the field of technology focus more on future predictions. The concern over the future of jobs under the influence of modern technology grows, while companies and employees wonder whether they'll be eventually replaced by machines.

We don't share that concern. We believe in the future of the human workforce and human value that machines will never replace. Here's why:

- Human value is an irreplaceable part of many industries;
- Natural interaction and man-to-man contact is necessary to keep the workplace mentally healthy;
- Machines aren't likely to replace fine motor skills;
- Product value in many industries comes from authentic human engagement, cultural aspects, and other non-tech factors;

Why Machines Won't Replace Human Workers

Computerization threatens to endanger nearly 47% of the jobs in the future, according to various statistic reports. Machine learning is bridging the gap between human knowledge and task performance. White-collar jobs are no longer safe, as machines become capable of performing simple and predictable tasks. There are some future predictions that even doctors will no longer be safe from automatization.

But, there are quite a bit of intriguing predictions when it comes to automating manual jobs. It seems that intellectual tasks are even easier to automate than manual because manual labor requires detailed motor skills. This requires far more computation and resource than intellectual tasks.

Automation Will Transform Jobs

Tasks related to customer service, trading, and shopping, tasks requiring physical labor, and AI-based technologies, require natural-looking interaction. All this thanks to the machine learning and language processing, which has a great impact on customer experience. However, machines are less likely to replace those customer service job posts where human interaction is an important part of the experience. For this reason, automating parts of the job so that an employee can spend more time making the customer experience more convenient is the likelier direction in which the companies will go.

How Future Predictions Affect Companies?

A business owner is unlikely to completely automate portions of jobs for decades to come. The sophistication and resources needed to put the digital vision in motion will require industries to invest more in human resource for the time being. Adapting employees to a new set of skills and hiring a workforce to cater to the customers in the best possible way remains a priority.

The future of jobs worldwide lays in the cooperation of machines and workers, where automation enhances and speeds up less relevant tasks so that the human brain can focus on those tasks with the highest priority.

Fair Hiring As the Future of Jobs

No matter what predictions are in terms of automation, companies must stay in the 'Now'. Instead of worrying about technology, they focus on keeping their business viable and growing so that it lives to see the future of technology. How does one do that? The future demands for business owners will likely move towards:

- Fairness in hiring;
- Fair distribution of resources and rewards;

● Understanding of customer's needs through diverse hiring;

● Hiring staff capable of growth and updating skills;

Jobs of the Future Rely On Personal Qualities

High paying jobs in demand for the future in various industries include supervisors, sales consultants, advisors, and many other occupations. These profiles all include a human factor that so far can't be replaced by machines.

Careers in demand for the future will also include medical practitioners and pharmacists, among many others. Experts who are capable of both diagnosing and treating medical conditions will be in demand, so the list of future jobs doesn't fall short on hundreds of thousands of posts.

Interestingly, a large number of these occupations doesn't even require a college degree. It seems that personal traits and manual skills will have the biggest impact on choosing the right people.

What about the Tech Industry?

Top IT jobs in demand for the future include a wide variety of profiles related to web development, app development, consulting, and management. Among projected IT jobs that will still exist in the future are those that are high in demand today, so it seems safe to say that IT jobs are one of those jobs that will never disappear.

How AI do help Recruit for Future Job Market

AI helps companies discover applicants who are:
- Strong-minded and creative;
- Aware of the importance of sustainability;
- Capable of learning and growing with the demands of the market;
- Great team workers;

With the knowledge of what jobs will there be in the future, AI blind hiring software offers companies the right tools to recruit exactly the profile of employees they need in order to take their business to the next level.

Four-dimensional education

Artificial intelligence for meta-learning

Knowledge skills and character + education meta-learning results in 4D Education. This is an "all-around concept" that ensures that students will not only adopt necessary information and skills, but also be able to associate the matter with higher-level thinking, resulting in forming conclusions, values, and principles that will make them more aware not only of their personal growth but also ideas for social improvement.

Current learning

At the current time, educational systems focus on studying information that revolves around certain fields of expertise. Subjects and lessons are the information that students are supposed to sync and retain. Students are also expected to form skills through training which means that the overall situation in education is that it affects only one aspect of the personality- the professional. However, in order to truly advance education, one must approach learning from all levels of personality. In the future of tasks related to different occupations by machines and artificial intelligence, the role of a human will be to the focus on enhancing social justice and quality of life.

Demands of societal changes

Nowadays the majority of people in the world have sufficient food and means for life. Still, the societal demands are greater. Moreover, people are faced with more need for personal improvement rather than professional. There is a need for mindfulness, need for empathy, and need for more social engagement. That requires learning of all of the values that current educational systems fail to include in subjects and lessons.

Future learning

Future learning will be oriented towards information, knowledge, and skills as a lot of them will be replaced by machines. Humans will have to make a switch to essentially give these basic tools a higher purpose and to use them purposefully to battle social injustice. This is where AI comes in as a transformative tool to ultimately change the world and mankind.

Meta-learning

Human brain runs constantly. This process is almost unconscious. On a very basic level learning is receiving information, analyzing it, making connections and associations as well as forming conclusions and skills based on it. However, meta-learning is the highest level of learning. Meta-learning means becoming aware of your own learning path. It means becoming self-aware of a personal transformation. Artificial intelligence allows people to focus more on personal growth and personal progress, and not so much on forming the very basic tools and skills required to do their professional tasks.

Unlike today's educational systems, the future in which the artificial intelligence is a basic tool in the process of learning is the future in which we will no longer spend so much time building the basic professional skills. Students will be faster at building skills and will focus more on personal growth and putting in more effort into making progress and revolutionary results with our knowledge. This is so-cold "forward learning: and it is one of the possibly most valuable and most beneficial forms in which machine learning take over a significant portion of what education is today.

Future learning and overcoming employment bias

The reason companies are to blame for the slow growth of their business is that they are losing talent. Despite investing hundreds of thousands, or even millions of dollars yearly on Human Resources and fair recruiting, businesses are still at a loss. Why? The answer is the subconscious brain and the way it sabotages fairness and equality in the workplace.

Unconscious bias is always at work in the mind of every person alive. It's not one's attitude that's the problem or their political views. A recruiter can be the most tolerant, the most politically correct person walking the Earth, and they'll still be biased when hiring. Unconscious bias shapes not only impressions but more importantly, expectations. The conclusions about the person's level of expertise aren't the problem. The expectations of a person, on a subliminal level, are the problem.

Despite all of the knowledge, companies worldwide expect more from mid-age white men than they do from women or workers of color. The moment a brain detects a specific feature in a person, it results in increasing or lowering expectations. As a result, companies are most likely to hire people from whom they feel like they can expect the most performance. They're often wrong. The employees notice these tendencies and perceive the employer as being less fair than they are.

Fairness in the Workplace: The Definition

So, what is fairness at work? What are the things that go into the fair treatment of employees in the workplace? There are three main forms of fairness employees look at:

- Distributive Justice;
- Procedural Justice;
- Interactional Justice;

Distributive Justice

How fair companies are in paying workers? How often workers receive praise? Employees who feel unappreciated find it hard to be loyal and engaged with the company. The more complex the company structure is, and the bigger the number of employees, the harder it becomes to track employee satisfaction. Treating employees fairly and equally will motivate loyalty, but those companies that treat employees fairly but not equally risk being perceived as discriminatory and biased.

Procedural Justice

Are companies fair in distributing the company resources to employees? Are they falling victim to gender or racial profiling? Employees seem to have the strongest reaction to being judged based on criteria that don't have to do with their skills or performance. Despite millions of dollars invested in workplace equality, 80% of workers nationwide are dissatisfied with their jobs. As a result of that, companies are losing between $450 and 500 BILLION on a yearly level.

The subconscious mechanisms of profiling and stereotyping have a long evolutionary history. Their role is primal, to identify with one's own uninformed group in order to stay safe. Thousands of years since the time these mechanisms served us well, we are still battling them. Now, they are doing employers worldwide a disservice. Subconscious bias is making recruiters look over genuine skill, talent, and personality and judge by hairstyle, tattoos, and speech accent.

Sadly, those who suffer the most due to this type of bias are employees who don't fit the standard profile and educational background. Most of the workers who get unfair treatment are:

- Racial minorities;
- Ethnic minorities;
- Women;
- Young and elderly of all backgrounds;

What is making workers disloyal?

Long hours, questionable contracts, and lasting fear of job loss cause employees to view the company as a bad employer. From a business point of view, keeping one's options open and nurturing a competitive environment is a good way for employees to stay on their toes. But it has a complete opposite impact on a business. Companies are losing talent and profits because employees don't feel safe. Treating employees fairly and consistently, without discrimination based on contracts, is one of the ways to ensure loyalty.

Contract inequality, especially between the agency and long-term employees, leads to less drive and engagement from agency workers. Offering equal contracts and a fair chance to everyone ensures the employee motivation and drive to contribute to company growth.

Interactional Justice

Are employees treated with dignity? Is there fairness in acknowledging achievements, rewarding engagement, and sanctioning the opposite?

Justice at work is one of the most influential factors that determine employee satisfaction and engagement. How does treating all employees equally benefit a company? Fairness in the interactions at work affects:

- Employee Engagement
- Trust
- Commitment in employees.

Workplace Fairness and AI

Employees are most loyal to those employers who provide:

- Fair procedures in distributing rewards.
- Detailed and accurate explanations for outcomes.
- Tailored communication to meet the employee's needs.

How Can Employers Become Fair With Artificial Intelligence

Biased expectations are and always will shape the perception of employees. Workers will be most loyal if they feel appreciated, valued, and secure. Your human brain isn't likely to abandon bias anytime soon, so AI, through the hiring software, offers a solution.

AI in recruitment can provide:

- Detecting real talent over flashy resumes;
- Completely unbiased hiring that will earn you a great reputation;
- Company growth with right people on your team;

Blind hiring is the only way to ensure the right work team structure and personality traits that are in the company's best interest. With the use of AI in recruitment, the applicants, workers, and team members will know that companies have their best interest at heart. Using blind hiring, you will not only get the best of the best in terms of skill and team structure. You will earn credibility in the employee's eyes, which will result in higher engagement and more profits.

Unbiased Recruiting With AI Helps Boost Talent and Increase Workplace Diversity

Can companies ensure fair recruiting practices? Many recruiters are unaware that it takes them less than a minute to make a decision based on a resume. They might not be aware, but the unconscious bias is costing companies billions of dollars in profits every single year.

Despite best efforts, recruiters are making assumptions on job applicants based on their gender, race, educational background, location, and appearance. Research showed that these irrelevant factors can increase or reduce the applicant's chance of getting a job by 50%. It's not only the negative bias that's affecting companies. Positive presumptions about candidates are harmful as well. A recruiter is most likely to think highly of a candidate with more experience or the one with a prestigious educational background. None of these details guarantee that the person will do their job well, nor that they will be a good member of the team.

Unconscious bias in recruiting affects:

- Overall company performance, including the performance of teams and individuals.
- Work environment and morals.
- Employee motivation.
- Talent.
- Finances of the company.
- Hiring decisions.
- Fairness in compensation and distribution of company resources.
- Promotion decisions.

- Rewarding and sanctioning criteria.

As a result of biased hiring, recruiters are not paying enough attention to the exact skills required for the job. They are not seeing if the applicant possesses not only the right skills but also the right personality traits to work on the team. As a result, the existing employees feel unappreciated. They notice the subtle differences in treatment, and the best of your workforce is looking for better opportunities. Not only that, but recruiters are most likely to hire less competent applicants and those who aren't true team players. This leads to the unproductive and hostile work environment. Safe to say, when employees aren't satisfied, the company isn't profiting.

Solution: Blind Hiring through AI Software

Blind hiring is a process that uses the tools that eliminate personal details about applicants and test skills and personality instead. Blind hiring tools hide:
- Name and address of the applicant;
- Age and gender;

- Accent and skin color;
- Educational background;
- Years of experience;

Is blind hiring the best hiring?

The biggest benefit from blind hiring for companies is the possibility to choose applicants solely based on talent.

It's safe to say that blind hiring is the future of recruitment. Companies will benefit the most from blind hiring if they combine it with a gender-neutral, unbiased, job description. Designing a job description that is inclusive in the formulation will help you draw a diverse group of applicants. Subtle messages passed through job descriptions can make certain minority groups feel like they don't belong to the company. Example: 'Strong' might drive away people who don't identify with an aggressive attitude, but 'Person of integrity' is a more inclusive option. The biggest benefit from blind hiring for companies is the possibility to choose applicants solely based on talent.

What Are the Greatest Benefits of Blind Recruitment?

Name-blind recruitment ensures that applicant's coming from minority backgrounds get an equal chance. With name blind hiring, it is virtually impossible to detect and judge based on ethnicity or cultural factors.

Blind resume software will blur out all of the details from a submitted resume that reveals gender, educational background, travel distance, and other factors irrelevant to skills that might affect a recruiter. During a blind resume review, recruiters can only observe details relevant to the job application.

Blind Hiring Limitations

Most blind hiring statistics show higher-quality teams and better work results that come from hiring based on skills and favorable personality traits. However, blind hiring doesn't always result in greater diversity. In some companies, blind recruiting led to the complete opposite outcome than predicted. It turned out that fewer women and minorities passed the blind tests. This led experts to further study the formulations of job description and expectations. It was revealed that wording, particularly in the aspect of personal traits, had a big role in excluding minority groups. For example, if the post required applicants to recognize themselves as "driven", and the applicants came from a cultural background where modesty is a desired quality, they were less likely to stay motivated to proceed with the application.

Pros and Cons of Blind Hiring

Here's a breakdown of some of the blind hiring pros and cons:

Pros:

● Supports hiring based on talent and skills;

● Improves company reputation;

● Helps form a high-functioning work team;

● Helps create a positive work atmosphere;

● Help reduce discrimination or discrimination based complaints during the hiring process.

● Confidence boost with talent and less doubt

● Direct impact on company morale and profit.

Cons:

● If not combined with unbiased job descriptions, blind hiring can result in less diversity.

Blind hiring is the future of recruitment. It is a solution for both job seekers and employers to ensure talent and skill-based hiring. Blind hiring is THE strategy to overcome the challenges of discrimination and create a truly diverse work environment.

E-Learning and Social learning: Bridging the Gap between Isolated Virtual Environments and Natural Tendencies for Environmental Learning

Can digital learning environments secure all the intangible, spontaneous influences a developing mind needs to build social skills and self-awareness? For a more in-depth analysis, one must think of learning as a process that goes beyond the individual minds and has important social aspects that we must not ignore.

The interest in the role of social interaction in the learning process grows with interest in the work of Vygotsky, Piaget, and Bandura, as well as studying the relationships of the individual with her social environment.

In this context, learning is seen as a set of individuals' interactions with the social environment, starting from informal forms of learning and development that begin from birth to a process of learning in formal education systems, along with informal and informal forms of acquiring knowledge, skills and habits in everyday interaction with a social environment.

Social Skills & Community

One of the most common forms of social learning is when the community help individuals to gain knowledge. This knowledge isn't only factual, but also cultural in nature. Moreover, individuals tend to gain a greater amount of knowledge through unconscious than through continuous forms of learning. In this sense, children and young adults Meta-Learning about social norms and desired/accepted behaviors in schools and from everyday experiences. Although not explicitly a part of curricular activities, these unconscious "lessons" are what shapes a student's mind in both positive and negative ways.

Forms of environmental learning are numerous, from teaching in school by teachers to receiving instructions from officials in institutions. In the context of machine learning, collaborative learning in the form of teamwork assists individual learners in problem-solving and knowledge building.

Learning through Social Mediation

It is suggested that the presence of a "social agent" in the computerized education should be introduced to assist the student in overcoming obstacles. Although learning through social mediation can work similarly to receiving instructions, the difference is that instruction in its classical form does not offer to learn through the help of others.

In this sense, we can discuss the possibility of instructively designed digital learning environments to provide students with adequate learning in the community. Learning can also be seen as a process of participation in the social process of constructing knowledge. These systems are highly integrated and situational, and interaction is socially divided. This is different from individual tutoring and team solving.

The cultural context is related to the search for literature and tools that are instilled with cultural heritage. In that sense, students can form an intellectual partnership in problem-solving. This form of learning acknowledges the specific cultural patterns, setting up the hypothesis and the process of thinking and analyzing. E-learning systems provide these requirements through opportunities for working together and advising students through discussion boards and forums.

Cultural Heritage as a Hidden Influence

Cultural heritage is an important learning factor that carries hidden, unconscious assumptions and calls to action, influencing decisions about the pace and the form of achieving certain goals.

Social identity as a system of learning encompasses collective efforts in acquiring knowledge and skills through retaining patterns of student behavior. Many actions that take place make sense within the framework of collective work while losing it from an individual standpoint. For this reason, it is essential to structure and make transparent all the important requirements and learning circumstances.

Social Learning & Meta-Learning

Learning to learn is a fundamental aspect of learning. Meta-learning is increasing in importance and interest in numerous sciences, blending psychology, anthropology, and sociology with IT.

The field of 'metamemory' studies memory and memory management. One of the forms of this learning is learning to speak for help and forming a habit of giving help. In this context, the individual in a group of students develops awareness of the necessity of providing and seeking help in the learning process.

Social content includes matters such as agreeing with others, maintaining assertiveness, cooperating in decision making and implementing actions.

Developing communication & Moral Skills

Education has a more informative context and the use of technologies threatens to endanger the professional ethos, according to many researchers. Difficulties arise from the barrier of incorporating legal values in the cultural and professional context in the form of computerized education.

Namely, some of the reasons that computerized training represents a challenge in the context of the education of legal professionals are the absence of the formation of adequate communication skills, which are the basis of most professions.

The explanation for this lies in the flexibility of computerized education, which in this case represents the paradigm. On the one hand, this flexibility yields some efficiency and learning comprehension, while on the other hand, it reflects the formation of communication skills necessary for dealing with the legal profession.

Metacognitive Learning Awareness

Effective learning involves synchronized functioning of different systems organized into reciprocal spirals, with multiple instruction systems dependent on the design of the instruction, including the reciprocal interaction of students with teachers and learners with content.

Learning largely depends on self-regulation and self-medication or mediation through another agent. There's a lack of metacognitive awareness of one's own learning in institutional school education, while the learning process is more effective in environments where individuals within the group direct their own learning and the learning of other members.

Higher-Order Learning in Asynchronous E-Learning

Asynchronous e-learning can positively influence the achievement of effective higher-order learning through a rich cognitive presence.

Higher-order learning is shown in the dimensions of reflection, self-management, and metacognition. Under asynchronous learning, the author implies the possibility of collaborative learning of the personalized convenience of an individual, in a way that guarantees equally interaction and independence from the group.

This possibility did not exist in earlier forms of learning. Asynchronism and connectivity remain to be key features of computerized learning.

Targeted Instructions & Success Predictions

One study showed a weaker ability to predict learning outcomes and educational scenarios using dual encoding strategies, static presentations, representing uninteresting information, testing, and separation.

On the other hand, better predictions were demonstrated among students who received targeted instruction and those students who were directly exposed to those empirical studies from which the results were obtained.

This research suggests that college students are largely unaware of the strategies that could help them memorize course information. It has been found that training in memory strategies has potential opportunities to improve metacognitive abilities.

Since attendees of e-courses rely heavily on instruction in learning, they may lose the ability to self-regulate. Studies have shown that the lack of self-regulation in learning can lead to academic failure, while good self-regulators control one's own cognition, motivation, and behavior in order to achieve goals.

It is very important for the educational practice to build effective digital environments for self-regulation, which should contribute to the creation of friendly environments for machine learning, such as discussion boards and homework, in order to enhance students' motivation, in particular, internal motivation. Internal motivation affects satisfaction while external motivation depends on perceived utility. In order to make students more aware of the usefulness and satisfaction of machine learning, it is important to encourage their self-efficacy. The observed usefulness of machine learning is growing with the growing friendly environment of the environment.

Challenges of Grand-Scale E-learning and Opportunities for Improvement

Looking into the course of development of e-learning, there's a clear discrepancy in the level of scientific achievement through individual projects on the one end, and the possibilities for grand-scale implementation on the other.

To illustrate this, let's look at the communication and interaction in relation to machine learning, by including the elements of the implicit curriculum that affect the learning process.

The features of the virtual learning environment include:

- The characteristics of online teachers,
- The possibilities of interaction between students within the group,
- Collaborative work and problem-solving learning,
- The metacognitive aspect of learning and,
- The process of social learning which entails the cultural and class conditionality of learning;

Interaction as a Critical Factor in E-Learning

The learning process as a set of interactions between students and teachers, students and content, students with the group, students and systems, devise the overall didactic quadruple.

We have adopted a broader concept of learning, observing it as the totality of individual and external interactions. Computerized education, as a form of learning mediated by computerized media, carries with it numerous advantages and disadvantages compared with classical education characterized by direct communication between students and teachers and pupils among themselves.

Digital communication within e-learning environments carries numerous advantages, such as:

- Availability,
- Independence in relation to geographical location,
- Freedom from fear of authority,
- Networking and connectivity,

Thus providing opportunities for students of different social and cultural backgrounds to participate in the educational process.

What are The Shortcomings of E-Learning Environments?

However, we find that each of these advantages is accompanied by the equal amount of disadvantages, mainly arising from the distant and technical nature of the ICT in e-learning.

The wide availability of computerized education doesn't always guarantee equal opportunities for participation for all participants.

Internet/Technology Dependency

With the possibility of independence in relation to the geographic location, computerized education is conditioned by the Internet availability, availability of computers and related technologies, as well as the preparation of students to participate in the courses.

Student's Language Skills

Language skills are also a significant influence when it comes to participation in digital learning, with non-English speakers and those who studied English as a second language still showing a reduced capacity to fully comprehend digital learning materials.

Even with groundbreaking technological development of the modern era, not all of the necessary resources are available to students worldwide. The economic and institutional factors still limit equal access to e-learning resources across the globe. It's clear that, while e-courses have the potential to provide equal access to learning opportunities to all, regardless of geolocation and social status, internet access remains limited due to already mentioned factors.

The E-Learning Environment Design and Teacher Training

The e-learning outcomes are also heavily reliant on the design of e-learning environments, the teacher's personality and cultural heritage, as well as the skill level. While there are plenty of available resources for educating teachers to become e-teachers, adjusting to methods that are culture-neutral and may be deprived of non-verbal elements remains a challenge.

Let's not forget that teachers are the ones who are setting the overall classroom climate. In the big picture, securing equal learning opportunities within e-learning environments also means educating teachers to identify emotional states and the crisis in students from diverse backgrounds on the grand scale. Meaning, teachers need tools and training to be able to detect students who are falling behind before the crisis occurs.

As some of the negative outcomes due to an emotional crisis in e-students may include academic failure, errors in interpretation, and lack of motivation, adequate teacher training remains a crucial task for the future.

In addition, the barriers stemming from the lack of direct face-to-face communication are still present, despite the efforts to overcome miscommunication, through staff training.

Importance of non-verbal communication

Observed obstacles relate to the absence of nonverbal communication, its spontaneity, and the lack of communication between the participants themselves. Findings of research related to the interaction of participants in computerized courses, and teamwork in collaborative problem-solving, give inconclusive results.

On the one hand, it has been established that team learning and collaborative problem-solving in the communities of e-learning is achievable and can be effective, provided that it is adequately guided by the teacher and the virtual environment system itself.

However, this relates to the quality of content management, but, on the other hand, there is also research that speaks in favor of the presence of feelings of social isolation among the participants, the inability of mutual knowledge and progress comparison, and the reduced possibility of self-regulation in learning.

Social Learning & Social Skills

This directly relates to the possibility of social learning and metacognitive learning processes. Research has shown that the characteristics of the instructional design of the course, with the individual characteristics of students, greatly influence the metacognitive aspect of learning, and therefore the depth of the acquired knowledge.

It is also established the connection between the quality of knowledge, motivation and the notable importance of the course and the feeling of satisfaction with participation in it, for which the design and content of the course are the final factors in learning outcomes.

We devoted special attention to social learning as an uninterrupted and universal process that takes place in everyday life, through the life of an individual.

Learning from and through the community, which is present from birth, then learning through community participation, learning social content, learning by cultural design, learning to be a social learner and the presence of social identity as a learning system, are the aspects of learning where a great place for improvement remains, in terms of e-learning.

With all the efforts to introduce tools and opportunities for social interaction and participation in computerized learning platforms, these elements are something that remains to be questioned, as the area itself remains relatively poorly explored.

About the Author

To begin, Harib Shaqsy has been writing books for many years.

He brings over thirty years of practical knowledge in his books and does coaching from time to time.

He is the author of the best seller book "Hard Work Can Keep You Poor." In his book, Harib feels that most people are over working and over stressed unnecessarily, because, they believe that working hard is the only way to survive, be paid more and become richer, he explains why this is not true in his book.

You can also check some of Harib's work available in bookshops and online.

Visit website: http://haribshaqsy.com

References

Atwell G. & Costa C. (2009) Integrating personal learning and working environments. Beyond
Current Horizons. Available at:
www.beyondcurrenthorizons.org
Bransford, J. D., Brown, A., & Cocking, R. (2000). How people learn: Mind, brain, experience
and school, expanded edition. DC: National Academy Press, Washington.
Bresnen, M., Goussevskaia, A., & Swan, J. (2005). Organizational routines, situated learning
and processes of change in project-based organizations.Project Management Journal, 36(3), 27.
Bulatović, N., Stefanović, D., Mirković, M., & Ćulibrk, D. (2013). Primena sistema za elektronsko
učenje na visokoškolskim ustanovama u Srbiji–pregled aktuelnog stanja. Preuzeto sa:
http://infoteh.etf.unssa.rs.ba/zbornik/2013/radovi/RSS-4/RSS-4-1.pdf
Castañeda, L. y Adell, J. (2013). La anatomía de los PLEs. En L. Castañeda y J. Adell (Eds.),
Entornos Personales de Aprendizaje: Claves para el ecosistema educativo en red (pp. 11-27).
Alcoy: Marfil.
Chen, Y., Chen, N. S., & Tsai, C. C. (2009). The use of online synchronous discussion for
Web-based professional development for teachers. Computers & Education, 53(4), 1155-1166.

Cooze, M., & Barbour, M. (2007). Learning styles: A focus upon e-learning practices and their
Implications for successful instructional design.
Ćamilović, D. (2013). Visokoškolsko obrazovanje na daljinu. Tranzicija,15(31.), 29-39.
Dean, G. J., & Murk, P. J. (1998). Progress Town Analysis--An Application of the Process Model
for Experiential Learning in Adult Education.
Dewey, J. (1938). Experience and education. New York: Macmillan.
Dipietro, M. (2010). Virtual school pedagogy: The instructional practices of K-12 virtual school
Teachers. Journal of educational computing research,42(3), 327-354.
Ekwunife-Orakwue, K. C., & Teng, T. L. (2014). The impact of transactional distance dialogic
Interactions on student learning outcomes in online and blended environments. Computers &
Education, 78, 414-427.;
Fischer, F., & Waibel, M. C. (2002). Wenn virtuelle Lerngruppen nicht so funktionieren, wie sie
eigentlich sollten. Referenzmodelle netzbasierten Lehrens und Lernens. Münster: Waxmann.
Fresen, J. W. (2005). Quality assurance practice in online (web-supported) learning in higher
Education: An exploratory study (Doctoral dissertation, University of Pretoria).
Garrison, D. R. (2003). Cognitive presence for effective asynchronous online learning: The role
of reflective inquiry, self-direction and metacognition.Elements of quality online education: Practice and direction, 4, 47-58.

Glušac, D. (2012). Elektronsko učenje. Univerzitet u Novom Sadu, Tehnički fakultet „Mihajlo
Pupin "Zrenjanin.

Govindasamy, T. (2001). Successful implementation of e-learning: Pedagogical considerations.
The internet and higher education, 4(3), 287-299.

Graf, D., & Caines, M. (2001). WebCT exemplary course project. In WebCT User Conference,
Vancouver, Canada. Retrieved June (Vol. 28, p. 2004).

Gruenfeld, D. H., & Hollingshead, A. B. (1993). Sociocognition in Work Groups The Evolution of
Group Integrative Complexity and Its Relation to Task Performance. Small Group Research,
24(3), 383-405.

Gulati2004

Hall, R. (2009). Towards a Fusion of Formal and Informal Learning Environments: The Impact of
The Read/Write Web. Electronic Journal of E-learning, 7(1), 29-40. Preuzeto sa:
www.ejel.org/issue/download.html?idArticle=81

Hein, G. E. (1991). Constructivist Learning Theory, International Committee of Museum
Educators Conferance, Jarusalem Israel, 15–22 October.

Holotescu, C. (2015, October). A conceptual model for Open Learning Environments. In
Proceedings of International Conference on Virtual Learning.

Huang, H. M. (2002). Toward constructivism for adult learners in online learning environments.
British Journal of Educational Technology, 33(1), 27-37.

Hurst, C. E. (2015). Social inequality: Forms, causes, and consequences. Routledge.

Juwah, C. (Ed.). (2006). Interactions in online education: implications for theory and practice.
Routledge.
Khan, B. H. (2005). E-learning quick checklist. IGI Global.
Kopp,B. , Hasenbein, M. & Mandl, H. (2014), Case-based learning in virtual groups –
Collaborative problem solving activities and learning outcomes in a virtual professional training
Course, Interactive Learning Environments, 22:3, 351-372, DOI:
10.1080/10494820.2012.680964
Kolb, D. (1984). Experiential Learning: Experience as the Source of Learning and Development,
Englewood Cliffs, NJ: Prentice Hall.
Zona, K., Dragan, C., Aleksandar, J., Duško, R., & Igor, F. (2014). Virtuelno okruženje za
praktično učenje grafičkog dizajna na daljinu. In International Scientific Conference of IT and
Business-Related Research-SINTEZA (pp. 10-15308). Singidunum University.
Macfadyen, L. P., & Dawson, S. (2010). Mining LMS data to develop an "early warning system"
for educators: A proof of concept. Computers & education, 54(2), 588-599.
Marković, D. (2005). Šta je neformalno u neformalnom obrazovanju?.NEFORMALNO
OBRAZOVANJE U EVROPI, 10. Preuzeto sa: http://www.hajdeda.org.rs/08_download/nfo/nfo_u_evropi _publikacija.pdf#page=10
Masoumi, D. (2010). Critical factors for effective eLearning. Goteburg University.

McCabe, J. (2011). Metacognitive awareness of learning strategies in undergraduates. Memory & Cognition, 39(3), 462-476.

Mikropoulos, T. et al, 1999. Picture: Virtual Reality into the Support of the Subject of Technology – Pedagogical Approach. Proceedings of the 4th Panhellenic Conference of Didactics of Mathematics and Informatics in Education. Rethymno, Greece, pp. 155-162

Milutinović, J. (2015). Kritički konstruktivizam-koncepcija i mogućnosti u oblasti obrazovanja. Nastava i vaspitanje, 64(3), 437-451.

Moore, M. G. (1989). Editorial: Three types of interaction.

Moore, K., & Iida, S. (2010). Students' perception of supplementary, online activities for Japanese language learning: Groupwork, quiz and discussion tools'. Australasian Journal of Educational Technology, 26(7), 966-979.

Mota, J. C. (2009). Personal Learning Environments: Contributos para uma discussão do conceito. Educação, Formação & Tecnologias-ISSN 1646-933X, 2(2), 5-21.

Oliveira, N. R., & Morgado, L. (2016), Personal Learning Environments: Research Environments and Lifelong Informal Learning, DOI:10.4018/978-1-4666-8803-2.ch00

Oliver, R. (2001). Strategies for Assuring the Quality of Online Learning in Australian Higher Education. In M. Wallace, A. Ellis & D. Newton (Eds). Proceedings of Moving Online II Conference (pp 222-231). Lismore: Southern Cross University.

Özgür, A., & Yurdugül, H. The investigation of learner-assessment interaction in learning
management systems. DODAJ

Papp, R. (2000). Critical success factors for distance learning" Paper presented at the Americas
Conference on Information Systems. Long Beach, CA, USA.

Pavičić Vukičević, J. (2013). Uloga implicitne teorije nastavnika u skrivenom kurikulumu
suvremene škole. Pedagogijska istraživanja, 10(1), 119-131.

Ragusa, A. (2010), Communication and social interactions in a technologicallymediated world,
Charles Sturt University, Australia, DOI: 10.4018/978-1-60566-874-1.ch001

Ramaprasad, A. (1983). On the definition of feedback. Behavioral Science,28(1), 4-13.

Riva, G., & Galimberti, C. (1998). Computer-mediated communication: identity and social
interaction in an electronic environment. Genetic, Social, and General Psychology Monographs,
124(4), 434.

Rodriguez, P., Ortigosa, A., Carro, R. (2014), Detecting and making use of emotions to enhance
student motivation in e-learning environments , Int. J. Cont. Engineering Education and
Life-Long Learning, Vol. 24, No. 2, 2014

Salomon, G., & Perkins, D. N. (1998). Individual and social aspects of learning. Review of
research in education, 23, 1-24.

Selim, H. M. (2007). Critical success factors for e-learning acceptance: Confirmatory factor
models. Computers & Education, 49(2), 396-413.

Schweibenz, W. (1998, November). The" Virtual Museum":
New Perspectives For Museums to
Present Objects and Information Using the Internet as a
Knowledge Base and Communication
System. In ISI (pp. 185-200).
Soong, M. B., Chan, H. C., Chua, B. C., & Loh, K. F. (2001).
Critical success factors for on-line
course resources. Computers & Education, 36(2), 101-120.
Thorne, S. L. (2003). Artifacts and cultures-of-use in
intercultural communication.Language
Learning and Technology, 7(2):33-67.
Thorne, S.L. and Payne, J.S. (2005). Evolutionary contractors,
Internet-mediated expression,
and language education. CALICO Journal, 22(3), 371-397.
Triantafyllidis, G. A., & Mitropoulou, V. (2005). CHANGING
CLASSROOM ENVIRONMENT BY
THE USE OF ICT AND THE NEW EMERGING ROLE OF THE
TEACHER.
Tuparova, D., & Tuparov, G. (2005). Didactical issues of e-
learning-Problems and future trends.
In International Conference on Computer Systems and
Technologies-CompSysTech.
Van Noy, M., James, H., & Bedley, C. (2016).
Reconceptualizing Learning: A Review of the
Literature on Informal Learning.
Vignjević, N. (2009). E-obrazovanje i sistemi za upravljanje
kursevima.
Volery, T., & Lord, D. (2000). Critical success factors in online
education.International journal of
educational management, 14(5), 216-223.
Vovides, Y., Sanchez-Alonso, S., Mitropoulou, V., & Nickmans,
G. (2007). The use of e-learning

course management systems to support learning strategies and to improve self-regulated
learning. Educational Research Review, 2(1), 64-74.

Vygotsky, L.S. (1978). Mind in society: The development of higher psychological processes.
Cambridge, MA: Harvard University press.

Wagner, E. D. (1994). In support of a functional definition of interaction.American Journal of
Distance Education, 8(2), 6-29.

Wang, T. H. (2008). Web-based quiz-game-like formative assessment: Development and
evaluation. Computers & Education, 51(3), 1247-1263.

Wang, T. H. (2010). Web-based dynamic assessment: Taking assessment as teaching and
learning strategy for improving students'e-Learning effectiveness. Computers & Education,
54(4), 1157-1166.

Waeytens, K., Lens, W., & Vandenberghe, R. (2002). Learning to learn': teachers' conceptions
of their supporting role. Learning and instruction, 12(3), 305-322.

Yurdugül, H., & Menzi Çetin, N. (2015). Investigation of the Relationship between Learning
Process and Learning Outcomes in E-Learning Environments. Eurasian Journal of Educational
Research, 58, 57-74.

Zimmerman, T. D. (2012). Exploring learner to content interaction as a success factor in online courses. The
International Review of Research in Open and Distributed Learning, 13(4),
152-165.